DRIVING SKILLS

D0514053

THE BUS & COACH DRIVING MANUAL

including the
Officially Recommended Syllabus
for the PCV Driving Test

London: HMSO

Written by Philip Welsh and Philip Martin with contributions from the staff of The Driving Standards Agency

Graphics by Vicky Squires of Squires Graphics, Chesterton, Cambridge.

Published by HMSO

© Crown Copyright 1995

First Published 1995

ISBN 0 11 551209 8

Applications for reproduction should be made to HMSO's Copyright Unit

Acknowledgements

The Driving Standards Agency would like to thank the following for their assistance in compiling this book.

The Association of Chief Police Officers of England, Wales and Northern Ireland

The Association of Chief Police Officers in Scotland

Phil Bowers and the Staff of Greater Manchester Metro Limited

The British Bus Preservation Group

Bus and Coach Training Limited, Rickmansworth

The Confederation of Passenger Transport UK

Michael Coker, Warwickshire County Coroner

The Convention of Scottish Local Authorities

The East Yorkshire Motor Services Group

Denis Foran and the Midland Fox Driver Training School

Hampshire Transport Management

The London Regional Passengers Committee

The Metropolitan Police Service

The National Federation of Bus Users

The National Playbus Association

Northampton Transport Limited (Grampian Regional Transport Group)

Northumbria Motor Services Ltd

Ian Norwell and Mercedes Benz (UK) Ltd

The 154 Preservation Society (Northampton)

The Passenger Transport Executive Group

Bob Pilbeam and the Metropolitan Police Coach Advisory Service

The Road Operators' Safety Council

South Yorkshire Passenger Transport Executive

Stagecoach (South) Ltd

The Traffic Director for London

The Yorkshire Traction Company Ltd

The staff of the Department of Transport and its Agencies

This, the fifth book in the DSA's *Driving Skills* series, provides detailed professional guidance for the safe driving of buses and coaches. As the driver of a vehicle carrying passengers you accept responsibility for their safety. Whether you drive a minibus with 8 passengers, or a double-deck coach with 88 people, each one is relying on you to look after them.

I particularly welcome the guidance which this book offers to minibus drivers. We have taken a flexible approach to the licensing and testing of minibus drivers in the voluntary sector, so as to minimise the burdens placed on them. But any minibus driver who has children or other passengers entrusted to his or her care has special responsibilities. This book provides an officially recommended syllabus plus a structured approach to training that should help you to be a safer driver.

As Minster for Road Safety I want every journey on the road to be a safe one. Driving standards are the key to achieving that. Buses, coaches and minibuses make many millions of safe and efficient journeys in Britain every year. Each one is dependent on the ability of the driver.

I am confident that studying this book will help you achieve a better understanding of the skills and attitudes which combine to make for higher driving standards.

Steven Norris
Minister for Local Transport and Road Safety

About this book

The Bus and Coach Driving Manual is about driving the many different types and sizes of passenger carrying vehicles – buses, coaches, minibuses and trams.

The book has been written in four easy-to-read parts in the established DSA style, with lots of illustrations.

Part 1 Learning to Drive a PCV

PCV drivers need to be thoroughly professional in their approach. This part of the book will help you understand the range of knowledge that a newcomer to PCV driving needs to acquire. It will also show what skills need to be learned in order to drive competently and safely.

Also explained is how to obtain a provisional PCV licence and the essential differences between driving cars and larger vehicles.

The importance of the correct attitude to driving and differing vehicle characteristics are also covered. Chapter 7 contains the officially recommended syllabus for the PCV driving test.

Part 2 The PCV Driving Test

Chapters 8 and 9 tell you how to apply for the test and what to expect on it.

Part 3 Driving PCVs

This part of the book gives advice on defensive driving, as well as driving in various weather conditions, at night and on motorways. It also deals with accidents and breakdowns.

Part 4 Additional information.

The DSA Service Standard, Complaints Guide and Compensation Code are in Part 4 of the book. Useful addresses and other helpful information can also be found in this part.

Reading this book will help you appreciate the principles of driving PCVs and become a safer driver.

Contents

Contents

Part 2
The Passenger Carrying Vehicle (PCV) Driving Test *87*

Contents

Contents

1. Applying for a provisional PCV licence entitlement

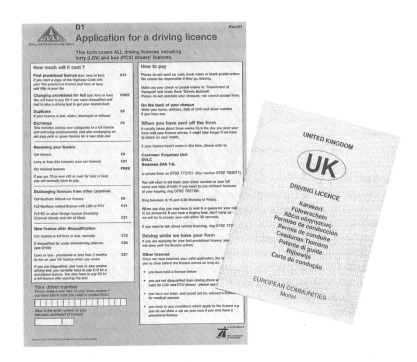

This chapter of the book explains what you need to do to obtain the licence entitlement to drive PCVs.

You must apply to the Driver and Vehicle Licensing Agency (DVLA) Swansea for provisional PCV entitlement to be added to your full car (category B) licence, unless you have held the entitlement before. You must not drive a PCV until you have received your licence with the category added. (See page 222)

1

Licence requirements

If you are unsure of the category of licence entitlement you need, refer to Chapter 18 of this book.

To be issued a licence to drive PCVs you must:

- be at or above the minimum age for the category of vehicle you intend to drive (see page 73)
- have a full driving licence entitlement for category B vehicles*
- meet the medical requirements (see page 3)
- pay the fee.

Completing the licence application form (D1)

You can obtain a driving licence application form (D1) from:

- Post Offices
- Traffic Area Offices (TAOs)
- Vehicle Registration Offices (VROs)
- DVLA Customer Enquiries Unit, DVLC, Swansea SA6 7JL.

Read the notes which accompany the form carefully.

If your category B licence is restricted to automatic vehicles, you can only drive a PCV with an automatic gearbox. If you want to drive a PCV with a manual gearbox you will have to pass a test in a car or a lorry with a manual gearbox*.

Fill in all relevant parts of form D1. The form may have to be returned to you and there may be a delay in issuing your licence if you leave anything out.

Where to apply

Send the completed form and everything you are asked to send with it to:

DVLC
SWANSEA
SA99 1BR

What to send

- The completed application form and
- your full category B car driving licence

or

- your provisional car driving licence and a valid driving test pass certificate (form D10)

and

- a completed medical report form (D4) signed by a doctor

and

- the appropriate fee*.

Further help

If you need advice about completing the form ring the enquiry number for DVLA listed on page 220 of this book.

---

* You are not allowed to drive PCVs which require category D, D1 or D (restricted) entitlement unless you have a full category B licence. Since 1990 it has not been possible to take a driving test on a bus without having previously passed a car test.

* If a vehicle has a clutch pedal it is classified as having a manual gearbox. Vehicles having fully automatic, semi-automatic, pneumocyclic, electronically controlled or pre-select gearboxes with a gearchange pedal, are all classified as automatic.

* The current fees and ways to pay are listed on the application form.

Driving a Passenger Carrying Vehicle carries a heavy responsibility to your passengers and other road users and it is vital that you can meet exacting standards.

Your eyesight must be of a much higher standard than that required of ordinary drivers.

You must be fit and free from any medical condition which could affect your ability to retain control of a bus or coach.

Eyesight Requirements for PCV Drivers

All drivers, for whatever category of vehicle, must be able to read a number plate at 20.5 metres (67 feet) in good daylight. If glasses or contact lenses are needed to do this, they must be worn while driving.

In addition

- an applicant who has not held a goods vehicle or bus licence before must have

    – a visual acuity of at least 6/9 in the better eye

and

    – a visual acuity of at least 6/12 in the other eye.

He or she must also have satisfactory uncorrected visual acuity.

Any applicant who has uncorrected acuity of less than 3/60 in both eyes will not be able to meet the required standard.

A driver who has an uncorrected acuity of less than 3/60 in one eye may be able to meet the required standard and should check with

DVLA
The Drivers' Medical Unit
Swansea SA99 1TU.

An applicant or licence holder who held a PCV/LGV licence before 1 March 1992 but who does not meet the standard above may still qualify for a licence. Information about the standard for such an applicant can be obtained from the DVLA Drivers' Medical Unit.

Where medical considerations include a relevant date, DVLA will make enquiries to establish the licensing position of all applicants at the date(s) in question.

An applicant or licence holder failing to meet the epilepsy, diabetes or eyesight regulations must by law be refused a licence.

If you only have eyesight in one eye you must declare this on Form D1.

Your doctor will use the standard Snellen test card to test your eyesight.

At the time of going to press changes were being planned for 1 July 1996. These will probably require higher standards from both new and existing drivers, the most significant of which are

- that uncorrected acuity of 3/60 will be required in both eyes
- drivers must have normal vision in both eyes (defined as a 120 degree field)
- there must be no evidence of double vision (diplopia).

Medical Examination and Form D4

You will need to have medical report form D4 completed and have a medical examination if this is your first application for PCV entitlement.

Form D4 must be completed by a doctor.

You will also need one if you are renewing your PCV licence and you are aged 45 or over unless you have already sent one to DVLA during the last 12 months.

Consult your doctor first if you have any doubts about your fitness.

You should only complete the applicant details and declaration on page 6 (Section 8) when you are with your doctor at the time of the examination. Your doctor has to witness you doing so.

This report is not available free under the National Health rules.

Your doctor is entitled to charge the current fee for this medical examination.

You are responsible for payment of the fee. It cannot be recovered from DVLA.

The fee is not refundable if your application is refused.

The completed form must be received by DVLA within 4 months of your doctor signing it.

Study the notes on pages 1 and 2 of the form. Remove them after the medical examination, and before sending in your application.

Your doctor will complete Sections 1 to 7.

Section 1 Vision
Is your eyesight good enough?

Section 2 Nervous System
Is there a history or evidence of any disease or illness affecting the nervous system?

Section 3 Diabetes Mellitus
Are you diabetic and, if so, is it controlled satisfactorily?

Section 4 Psychiatric Illness
Is there any evidence of psychiatric illness which may affect your ability to drive PCVs?

Section 5 General
Other medical conditions which may affect your work.

Section 6 Cardiac
Your heart and the systems it affects.

Section 7 Medical Practitioner Details

Medical Standards

You **may** be refused a PCV driving licence if you suffer from any of the following

- liability to Epilepsy/Seizure
- diabetes requiring insulin (unless you held a licence on 1 April 1991 and the Traffic Commissioner who issued that licence had knowledge of your condition)
- visual defects (see eyesight requirements above)
- heart disorders
- persistent high blood pressure
- strokes/unconscious lapses within the last 5 years
- any disorder causing vertigo within the last 2 years
- severe head injury with serious continuing after effects, or major brain surgery
- parkinson's disease, multiple sclerosis or other 'chronic' nervous disorders likely to affect the use of the limbs
- mental disorders
- alcohol/drug problems
- serious difficulty in communicating by telephone in an emergency
- visual field defects.

Ask your doctor's advice.

This chapter is about keeping control of your vehicle at all times and caring for your passengers.

To drive a bus, coach or minibus you need to have the right skills and attitude. You should be able to apply the defensive driving techniques described in this book.

You need to make the safety and comfort of your passengers your primary concern.

You should also be concerned about your responsibility to other road users.

You must have high standards and a sense of responsibility, whether you are self employed or work for a company. You will still be responsible for the safety of passengers. Your company's good name will be at stake if you do not care for customers.

You must never allow safety to be put at risk. You must remember that

No risk is ever justified

You need to appreciate the differences between driving cars and driving larger passenger vehicles.

You should also understand something of the various laws of physics concerning forces at work on your vehicle and its passengers.

Professional Standards

The passenger transport industry is subject to a wide range of regulations and requirements relating to

- drivers
- operators
- companies
- vehicles
- passengers
- workshops etc.

To become a professional bus, coach or minibus driver you will need a thorough knowledge of the regulations which apply to your work. You will also need a comprehensive knowledge of *The Highway Code*, including the meaning of traffic signs and road markings (especially ones which indicate restrictions for large vehicles).

Most importantly you will need to have a high level of driving skill.

The way you drive is vitally important.

- Drive properly and your passengers will arrive safely at their destination.
- Drive carelessly or dangerously and you risk the safety of your passengers and other road users.

If you act hastily, you risk endangering others. You need to constantly assess all the factors that might affect your task and plan your actions early.

If a bus or coach is involved in an accident there is bound to be damage, injury or loss of life. As a professional driver you have a part to play in making sure accidents don't happen.

90% of road accidents are due to human error. High quality training should help you avoid making such errors and reduce the risk of you becoming involved in accidents.

Sometimes accidents are due to mechanical failure of vehicle components. The way you drive can affect the life of these components. Drivers who demonstrate a high degree of what is called 'vehicle sympathy' cut the risk of that happening.

You are the one responsible for driving your vehicle safely and sensibly at all times.

1

Be a credit to yourself, your company and your profession.

Nowadays, there is a lot of competition for passengers. Such competition helps to ensure that high quality services are available. It also means that operators have to have tight cost controls to ensure efficient and effective use of their resources.

But cutting corners on safety is not acceptable and could be a recipe for disaster. For example:

- you must not drive a vehicle knowing it to have a serious defect

- if you are delayed do your best to make up time, but do not speed or take risks

- obstructing and 'racing' other vehicles from another operator is inexcusable.

Becoming a PCV driver

Study the information in Chapter 6 which deals with vehicle characteristics. You will need to understand how various kinds of PCVs handle in order to drive them safely.

Articulated vehicles

Articulated buses and buses towing trailers are relatively rare in the UK.

The information in this book about driving articulated vehicles and buses towing trailers is included for drivers seeking a D + E entitlement.

From car to bus

To drive a bus safely you must first appreciate the main differences between driving larger vehicles and driving smaller ones.

These are

- weight
- width
- length
- height
- body overhang
- distance needed to pull up
- distance needed to overtake
- control needed when going downhill
- power needed to climb uphill
- the need to avoid any sudden changes of speed or direction.

Some of these aspects will be obvious from the moment you first start to drive a larger vehicle.

Other features will only become apparent once you have started to drive one.

The essential factor is to recognise that much more forward planning is needed to drive a bus, coach or minibus safely.

Part 1 Learning to drive a bus or coach

1 Understanding PCVs

This chapter looks at the effects of the various forces that act on a vehicle and its passengers. You should understand something of the effect that these forces will have.

A basic law of physics states that every body will remain at rest or travel at a constant speed in a straight line unless acted upon by an external force.

A bus, coach or minibus

- laden or unladen
- alone or towing a trailer
- articulated

travelling in a straight line under gentle acceleration is relatively stable.

When a vehicle

- accelerates
- brakes
- changes direction

forces are applied to it and its load. The more violent or sudden the change, the greater the forces.

Sudden, excessive or badly timed steering, braking and acceleration will introduce forces which affect the stability of the vehicle and can result in loss of control.

Steering should always be

- smooth
- planned
- controlled
- accurate.

Braking should always be

- progressive
- correctly timed
- smooth
- sensitive.

Acceleration should always be

- purposeful
- used to best economic advantage
- well planned
- considerate.

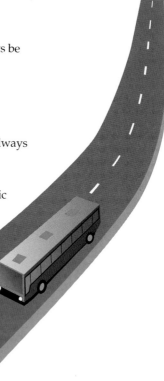

Keeping your passengers comfortable

Passengers have a choice. They can choose whether they have been looked after well enough on a journey to consider making another with the same operator. Operators publicise journeys as being comfortable and convenient, fast and trouble free. Drivers are important in delivering this sort of service.

Two almost identical vehicles from different companies operating the same route are at the bus stop together.

There are thirty people in the queue. Six get on the first bus and twenty four on the second one. The second one is behind, but still manages to pull away first, entirely as a result of good planning.

The driver of the second bus keeps 5p and 10p coins separately in her cash bag so she can give change to passengers quickly. Having left room to manoeuvre clear, she is able to pull away quicker, still smiling.

The other driver is chatting to his friend at the front of the bus and passengers have to ask twice for their tickets. He fumbles for the correct change, grumbling 'Have you got anything smaller?'

During your training, travel on the type of vehicles you will be using and look at how drivers treat you as a passenger. Learn from the best.

Keeping control

Make sure that you maintain control of yourself, your passengers and your vehicle. If you anticipate a problem try to plan a solution. Don't go blindly on hoping that it will sort itself out. Too many people rely on you.

1 Forces at work on your vehicle

Having looked at the care and comfort of your passengers, it is important to look now at how the forces acting on your vehicle can affect them.

Friction

This is the grip between two surfaces. The grip which the tyres have on the road surface transmits the force (traction) which is essential when

- moving away or accelerating
- turning/changing direction
- braking/slowing down.

The amount of grip will depend on

- the weight of the vehicle
- the speed of the vehicle
- the condition of the tyre tread
- whether the tyre is
  - under inflated
  - over inflated

- the type and condition of the road surface
  - loose
  - smooth
  - anti-skid
- weather conditions
  - fine and dry
  - rain
  - ice or snow
- any other material present
  - mud
  - wet leaves
  - diesel spillage
  - other slippery spillages
  - inset metal rails
  - loose road surfaces
- whether the vehicle is braking or steering sharply
- the condition of steering and suspension components.

Sudden acceleration or braking can lead to loss of friction between the tyre tread and the road surface.

Under these conditions the vehicle may

- lose traction (wheelspin)
- break away on a turn (skid)
- not stop safely (skid)
- overturn.

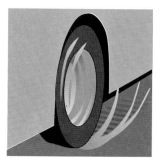

The same will happen when changing into a lower gear if travelling too fast, or if the clutch is suddenly released, because the braking effect will only be applied to the driven wheels.

Inertia and momentum

A stationary bus with 70 or 80 passengers on board may weigh up to 18 tonnes. It requires a great deal of force to make it begin to move, even on a flat road. But it takes relatively little power to keep it rolling at a constant speed. Resistance to movement is called inertia and the force which keeps the vehicle rolling is called momentum.

Modern buses and coaches have engines with a high power output to:

• give good acceleration

• overcome inertia.

Passengers are also affected by these forces. A passenger's inertia has to be overcome in much the same way as the vehicle's. Acceleration will push them back into their seats, while braking will move their weight forward due to momentum. Sudden braking will cause passengers to fly forward and could be dangerous.

All acceleration and braking should therefore be as smooth, controlled and progressive as possible.

The energy that is stored up in the vehicle and its passengers when travelling is known as kinetic energy. When braking this is converted into heat at the brake shoes and drums.

Continuous use of the brakes results in them becoming over-heated and losing their effectiveness (especially on long downhill gradients).

This is known as brake fade.

Timing

Much more effort is needed to stop a fully laden PCV than an ordinary car travelling at a similar speed. It is therefore important to avoid harsh braking. Plan ahead and take early action.

1

Gravity

When a vehicle is stationary on level ground the only force acting upon it is the downward pull of gravity (ignoring wind forces and so on).

- On an uphill gradient the effects of gravity will be much greater so that
  - more power is needed from the engine to move the vehicle forward and upward
  - less braking effort is needed and the vehicle will pull up in a shorter distance.
- On a downhill gradient the effects of gravity will tend to
  - make the vehicle's speed increase
  - require more braking effort
  - increase stopping distances.

Centre of Gravity

The vehicle's centre of gravity is the point around which all its weight is balanced.

All passenger vehicles are 'tilt tested' to ensure the design is stable. But violent steering, acceleration or braking moves the centre of gravity and places excessive forces on the vehicle's tyres and suspension and on the passengers. Heavy braking whilst cornering can bring components very close to their design limits and will be uncomfortable for passengers. Catching a kerb or raised manhole cover with a tyre under that sort of pressure could result in a blowout and the vehicle going out of control or even overturning.

Centrifugal force

When a vehicle takes a curved path at a bend the forces acting upon it tend to cause it to continue on the original straight course. This is known as centrifugal force.

At normal speeds this is overcome by the traction between the tyres and the road surface.

If a bus or coach takes a bend too fast, centrifugal force will cause the passengers to be thrown towards the outside of the bend.

Keeping control of your vehicle

When driving

- you cannot alter the severity of a bend
- you cannot change the weight of the bus and its passengers
- you cannot alter the design and performance characteristics of your vehicle and its components

But you do have control over the speed of your vehicle and the forces acting upon it.

Loss of Control

If you ask too much of your tyres by turning and braking at the same time, you will lose some of the available power and grip.

If the tyres slide or lift you will no longer be in full control of the vehicle.

To keep control

- Ensure all braking is
  - controlled
  - in good time
  - made when travelling in a straight line wherever possible.
- Reduce speed and, where necessary, select the appropriate gear BEFORE negotiating
  - bends
  - roundabouts
  - corners.

- Avoid braking and turning at the same time (unless manoeuvring at low speed)
  - reduce speed first
  - look well ahead to assess and plan.

Most of the forces described act on a vehicle in motion.

If you disregard them you will probably lose control.

Allow for them in your driving.

This book has already looked at your role in customer care, this chapter is concerned with your attitude whilst driving.

The general public tend to see the bus or coach driver either

- as a skilful professional who manoeuvres a large vehicle in difficult spaces and delivers passengers safely to their destination,

or

- as an impatient person determined to make other road users, and his passengers, do precisely what he wants them to.

As a PCV driver you want to create the best possible image by setting a good example for others to follow. Driving large vehicles can be very enjoyable and even more so when you can be proud that you are doing it well.

1

Driver Attitudes

You have a job to do. That is to get your passengers to their destination

- safely
- on time
- efficiently.

Safety

Chapter 3 discussed the forces acting on the vehicle and its passengers and how to control them safely. This chapter looks at how your driving behaviour affects safety.

The sheer size, noise and appearance of a typical PCV appears intimidating to cyclists, pedestrians and even car drivers.

When a bus or coach seems to be driven in an aggressive way, other road users can feel really threatened.

Tailgating

Tailgating involves a large vehicle (bus or lorry) travelling dangerously close behind another vehicle, at speed, with only a few feet between them. This often happens on motorways.

Not only are tailgating and driving in close convoy with other PCVs bad driving habits, but they often have serious consequences.

Some police forces are so concerned at the number of accidents involving tailgating vehicles that they now video and prosecute offenders.

Tailgating means that your view of the road ahead is seriously restricted and you are left with an impossible stopping distance.

Always maintain your safety margins. If a vehicle in front brakes heavily you need time to react and move your foot to the brake pedal. At 50 mph you will have travelled 15 metres (more than the length of a coach) before you can start to brake. During that time the vehicle in front could have reduced its speed to below 40 mph.

Considerate drivers also allow the driver following them ample time to react.

Speed Limiters

The introduction of speed limiters on coaches should have little effect on professional drivers. These devices merely prevent the vehicle exceeding the maximum motorway speed limit in this country (or 65 mph for international journeys from January 1995 and in the UK from January 1996).

Speed

You can never justify driving too fast just because you have to reach a given location by a specific time.

If an accident happens and you injure someone there is no possible defence for your actions.

You must not be tempted to drive faster when you are behind schedule.

Consider this example

Central London to Nottingham is about 130 miles. To average 50 mph with a coach is usually achievable with a relaxed driving style, bearing in mind that the first ten miles or so is through congested London traffic, and about 100 miles of the journey is by motorway.

Depart 8.00 am

Arrive 10.36 am

To average 55 mph is almost impossible and would certainly not be achieved with a relaxed driving style.

IF you managed to do it the result would be

Depart 8.00 am

Arrive 10.22 am

To gain less than a quarter of an hour would be at the expense of increased fuel costs and additional stress.

Would it be worth it ?

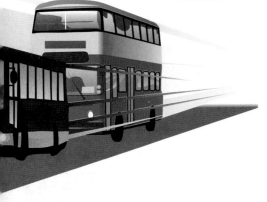

1

Intimidation

Never allow yourself to get into a situation where you are using the size, weight and power of your vehicle to intimidate other road users.

The repeated `hiss' of air brakes being applied or released while stationary gives the impression of 'breathing down the neck' of the driver in front.

Retaliation

You must resist the temptation to retaliate in order to

'teach someone a lesson'.

Always drive

- courteously
- with anticipation
- allowing for other road users' mistakes
- in full control of your vehicle.

You cannot act hastily when driving a PCV without the possibility of serious loss of control.

Effects of your vehicle

As a competent PCV driver you must always be aware of the effect your vehicle and your driving has on other road users.

You must recognise the effects of turbulence or buffeting your vehicle causes when overtaking

- pedestrians
- horse riders
- cyclists
- motorcyclists
- cars towing caravans
- cars
- other buses and lorries.

Smaller, lighter vehicles are also affected when they overtake you at speed, especially on motorways.

On congested roads, particularly in shopping areas, take extra care when you need to drive close to the kerb.

Be aware of

- pedestrians stepping off the kerb
- the danger of your nearside mirror striking the head of a pedestrian standing at the edge of the kerb
- cyclists moving up on the nearside of your vehicle in slow-moving traffic.

Courtesy and consideration

Courtesy and consideration are the hallmarks of a professional driver. Aim to be professional.

Neither the horn nor the headlights should be used to rebuke or to intimidate another road user.

Use of the horn

PCVs are often equipped with powerful horns and their use should be strictly confined to the guidance set out in *The Highway Code*. The horn is to warn other road users of your presence.

Never use the horn aggressively.

Do not use the horn between 23.30 hrs and 07.00 hrs in a built-up area, unless a moving vehicle poses a danger.

Use of the headlights

There is only one official use of flashing the headlights described in *The Highway Code*. That is to let other road users know you are there.

Never repeatedly flash the headlights while driving directly behind another vehicle.

To avoid dazzle do not put headlights on to full beam when following another vehicle.

Do not switch on auxiliary lights fitted to your vehicle unless weather conditions require them.

Misleading signals

By using unauthorised 'codes' of headlight or indicator flashing, you may be misunderstood by others. This in turn could lead to accidents. When driving abroad headlamp flashing is used purely as a warning. Any other intention will not be understood.

This chapter will help you understand what is involved in being a professional driver. It will also tell you what you need to know to be a safe and well informed driver.

The law does not accept ignorance as a defence. You need to know what your responsibilities are to yourself, your passengers, your employer (if you have one) and to other road users.

It is impossible to go into detail in the space available in this book so each topic is presented in outline. This will give you an idea of what you need to know. If you think you need more information talk to your trainer, or refer to other books and publications, to gain a fuller understanding.

Why not draw up your own checklist to record details about your vehicle, your route or the actions you must take to operate within the law, so that nothing is left to chance?

Basic knowledge

You need to know about the

- weight (for restrictions)
- height (for clearances etc.)
- width (for restrictions)
- length (lay-bys, corners)
- ground clearance (for hump-back bridges, grass verges, kerbs etc)

of your vehicle.

You will also need to know the various speed limits which apply to your vehicle and the speeds at which it will normally travel and cruise.

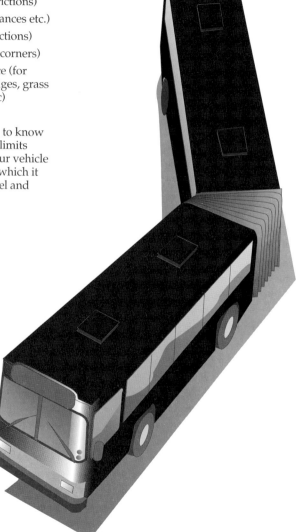

Weight limits

Weight limits are imposed on roads and bridges for two reasons

- the structure may not be capable of carrying greater loads
- to divert larger vehicles to more suitable routes.

Sometimes buses and coaches are exempted from notified limits by means of a plate beneath the weight limit sign. This normally means PCVs in service, or requiring to use the road for access. If you can use another route, do so. Try to be considerate towards local people and the environment.

Make sure you know what your vehicle weighs. Be aware of, and understand, the limits relating to any vehicle you drive.

In many cases weight limits apply to the maximum gross weight. Add about 1 tonne per 15 passengers to the unladen weight shown on your vehicle plus an allowance for any luggage you may be carrying.

For example

The weight difference between a laden and unladen coach may be as much as 7 tonnes.

75 seat double deck coach	12.0	tonnes
75 passengers	5.0	tonnes
75 cases	1.5	tonnes
500 litres fuel	0.5	tonnes
Total weight	**19.0**	**tonnes**

(Definitions of terms connected with weight limits are in the Glossary of Terms on page 234)

Height

You are not allowed to drive a vehicle which has an overall travelling height of more than 3 metres (10 feet) unless the overall travelling height (including any trailer) is conspicuously marked

- in feet and inches

or

- in feet and inches and in metres so that there is no more than 50mm difference between the height specified in feet and inches and the height specified in metres
- in figures at least 40mm high which can be read by the driver when in the driving position

and

- any height indicated is not less than the overall travelling height of the vehicle

and

- this is the only indication of the overall travelling height.

1

Overhead clearances

Drivers of any vehicle exceeding 3 metres in height should exercise care when entering

- loading bays
- bus and coach stations
- depots
- refuelling areas
- service station forecourts
- any premises which have overhanging canopies

or driving under

- bridges
- overhead cables
- overhead pipelines
- overhead walkways
- road tunnels.

The normal maximum permitted overall travelling height of any PCV with fixed bodywork is 4.88 metres (15'10").

Many countries in the European Community do not allow PCVs in excess of 4 metres without an exceptional vehicle permit being applied for, and issued, in advance.

Be aware of overhanging tree branches, particularly on roads rarely used by high vehicles, in case upper deck windows are broken. Trees on regularly used routes are generally kept trimmed. If in doubt, slow right down and, if necessary, stop, get out and check!

Don't take chances

All roads have a slope (camber) to help with drainage but this can cause problems. For example, on roads with a severe camber the top of a double deck bus can lean up to 25 cms further over than the wheels. This may be made worse when pulling up at bus stops if the nearside wheels drop into the gutter. Lamp posts, traffic signs, shop awnings, bus shelters and so on are within this 'danger zone' so watch out for these hazards.

Department of Transport and British Rail joint campaign to prevent 'Bridge Bashing'

1

Every year there are EIGHT HUNDRED accidents where vehicles hit railway or motorway bridges – some involving buses and coaches.

Collisions involving buses can kill or injure passengers and weaken the bridge. If a railway bridge is involved this would also disrupt rail traffic, or lead to a major disaster. Then there are the costs involved in making the bridge safe, re-aligning railway tracks and the general disruption to road and rail traffic.

The headroom under bridges in this country is at least 5.0 metres (16'6")

UNLESS OTHERWISE INDICATED.

Where the overhead clearance is arched this is normally ONLY between the limits marked.

1 If your vehicle collides with any bridge

STOP

Your first responsibility is to your passengers. Check there are no injuries. If there are take appropriate action (see page 201).

REPORT

If a railway bridge is involved you must report the incident to the Police and British Rail at the time.

If you do not report the incident at the time you must tell the Police within 24 hrs.

Failure to do so is an offence.

DO THIS IMMEDIATELY to avoid a possible serious accident and loss of life.

Never be tempted to 'Hit and Run.' The consequences are unthinkable.

Give information about

- the location
- the damage
- any bridge reference number (often found on a plate bolted to the bridge or wall).

You must know the height of your vehicle.

- Do not guess.
- Measure it, or look at the information shown in the cab.

Do not ignore

- traffic signs
- road markings
- warning lights.

Stay alert to the dangers!

Don't take chances

Height guide

Feet	Metres
16'6"	5.0
16'	4.8
15'	4.5
14'	4.2
13'	3.9
12'	3.6
11'	3.3
10'	3.0
9'	2.7

If you are not sure of the safe height STOP and call British Rail Works Group on 01345 581657 (All calls charged at local rate)

To avoid problems

- plan your route
- slow down approaching bridges
- know the height of your vehicle
- keep to the centre of arched bridges
- wait for a safe gap to proceed if there is oncoming traffic.

Width

You must always be aware of the road space your vehicle occupies.

This is particularly important where road width is restricted, because of parked or oncoming vehicles, or in narrow roads. The majority of buses and coaches in this country are 2.5 metres wide (8'3") but this can vary slightly between different makes. Mirrors and exterior trim can affect the vehicle's width.

Take particular care when meeting other large vehicles where space is limited. If necessary stop first and, if you are certain there is enough space, manoeuvre past slowly. Keep a look out all round and especially watch out for mirrors hitting each other, or lamp posts and so on.

A broken mirror means your vehicle is unroadworthy and, therefore, illegal. It can also cause injury to you or others.

Many local authorities now use 'traffic calming' measures which often include road width restrictions.

Watch out for them. If you know of roads with such restrictions, try to avoid them, unless of course you are following a scheduled service route.

Length

You need to know the length of your vehicle, as well as its width, so that you can judge the space you need on the road. You will also need to know these dimensions to comply with regulations that affect your vehicle.

Places where there are restrictions on vehicle length are comparatively rare. Examples are

- road tunnels
- level crossings
- ferries.

The usual maximum length for a bus or coach is 12 metres.

Passenger Carrying Vehicles exceeding 12 metres in length are restricted to the first 2 lanes of motorways with 3 or more lanes.

Articulated buses may be up to 18 metres long, although these require special dispensation.

Drivers of long vehicles must be careful when:

- turning left or right
- negotiating roundabouts or mini roundabouts
- emerging from premises or exits
- overtaking
- parking, especially in lay-bys
- driving on narrow roads where there are passing places
- negotiating level crossings (see pages 82 and 102 for detailed advice).

Be aware of the amount of space you need to turn (the 'turning circle') and the way your vehicle overhangs kerbs and verges (the 'swept area').

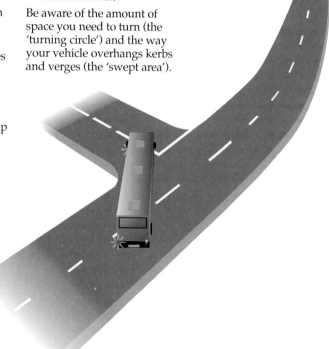

Vehicle Braking Systems

There are three braking systems fitted to PCVs

- The service brake
  - is operated by the foot control
  - is the principal braking system used
  - is used to control the speed of the vehicle
  - is used to bring it safely to a halt.
  - may incorporate an anti lock braking system (ABS).
- The secondary brake
  - may be combined with
    - the foot brake control or
    - the parking brake control
  - is provided for use in the event of a failure of the service braking systems
  - normally operates on fewer wheels than the service brake and therefore has a reduced level of performance.

- The parking brake
  - is usually a hand control
  - may also be the secondary brake but should normally only be used when the vehicle is stationary
  - must always be set when the vehicle is left unattended. (It is an offence to leave any vehicle without applying the parking brake).

Buses and coaches are frequently equipped with endurance braking systems (commonly called retarders).

Anti lock braking systems employ wheel speed sensors to detect the moment during braking when a wheel is about to lock. Just before this would happen the system reduces the braking effort and then rapidly re-applies it. This action may happen many times a second to maintain brake performance. Preventing the wheels from locking means that the vehicle's steering and stability is also maintained leading to safer stopping. ABS is only a driver aid. It does not remove the need for good driving practices such as anticipating events and assessing road and weather conditions.

Anti lock braking systems are in common use on large passenger carrying vehicles and are required by law on some. It is important to ensure that ABS is functioning BEFORE setting off on a journey. Driving with a defective ABS may constitute an offence. The satisfactory operation of the ABS can be checked from the warning signal on the dashboard. The way the warning lamp operates varies between manufacturers, but with all types the light comes on with the ignition and should go out no later than when the vehicle has reached a road speed of about 10 kph (6 mph).

Note: ABS is the Registered Trade Mark by BOSCH (Germany) for Anti Blockiensystem.

1 Endurance Braking Systems

Commonly referred to as retarders, these systems provide a way of controlling the vehicle's speed without using the wheel mounted brakes. This can be particularly useful when descending long hills when the vehicle's speed can be stabilised without using the service brake system. Braking generates heat in the brakes and, at high temperatures, braking performace can be affected. The retarder leaves the service brakes cold for good performance when required.

Retarders operate by applying a resistance via the transmission to the rotation of the vehicle's driven wheels. This may be achieved by

• increased engine braking

• exhaust braking

• transmission mounted electromagnetic or hydraulic devices.

The system may be operated

• in unison with the service brake control (integrated)

• by using a separate hand control (independent).

Retarders normally have several stages of effectiveness depending on the braking requirement. With independent systems the driver has to select the level of performance required.

When driving on slippery roads care must be exercised when operating independent retarders if rear wheel locking is to be avoided. Some retarders are under the management of the ABS system to help avoid this problem.

Safety

Air brake sytems are fitted with warning devices which will be activated when air pressure drops below a pre-determined level. In some circumstances there may be sufficient pressure to release the parking brake even though the warning is showing. Under these circumstances the service brake system may be ineffective. Therefore you should never release the parking brake when the brake pressure warning device is operating.

On some vehicles a special brake may be automatically applied when the vehicle is brought to a stop. This is designed to prevent the vehicle moving until the accelerator is used to move off. This is not a parking brake and you should not leave your seat until the parking brake has been applied.

Driver maintenance and inspection

You are not expected to be a mechanic. However, there are braking system checks that are the driver's responsibility.

Air reservoirs

Air braking systems draw their air from the atmosphere which contains moisture. This moisture condenses in the air reservoirs and can be transmitted around the vehicle's braking system. In cold weather this can lead to ice forming in valves and pipes and may result in air pressure loss and/or system failure. Some air systems have automatic drain valves to remove this moisture while others require manual draining daily. You should establish whether your vehicle's system reservoirs require manual draining and, if so, whose responsibility it is to make sure it is done.

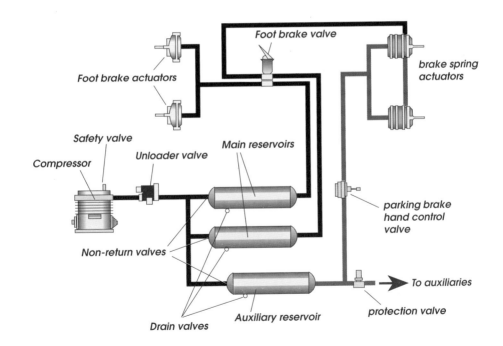

1

Controls

Before each journey make sure that all warning systems are working. Brake pressure warning devices can be activated by using a special 'check' switch. If ABS is fitted this should be done only when the ABS warning light is operating and, in any case, the ignition should be switched on first. Never start a journey with a defective warning device or when the warning is showing. If the warning operates when you are travelling, stop as soon as you can do so safely and seek expert assistance. Driving with a warning device operating may be very dangerous and is an offence.

Auxiliary air systems

Modern PCVs may be equipped with air operated accelerators, clutches, gear change mechanisms, wipers, doors, suspension, ramps, lifts or 'kneeling' devices. Operation of these may influence the vehicle's braking systems. Drivers should familiarise themselves with the function and effect of these systems and be aware of any 'interlinks' which may be fitted. (For example, where air operated accelerators are disabled when the passenger doors are open, etc.)

Power assisted steering (PAS)

Older and smaller vehicles have steering systems in which the effort the driver puts into turning the steering wheel is used to steer the front wheels. So that this effort is reasonable, a gearing system is used. The driver may need to turn the steering wheel several times to reach 'full lock' (the tightest turn the vehicle can make). With historic buses it is necessary to drive more slowly round corners just to give yourself enough time to turn the wheel.

In order to reduce the effort required and to limit the amount that the driver has to turn the steering wheel, many modern minibuses, buses and coaches are fitted with a power steering system. This uses an engine driven pump to supply hydraulic fluid under pressure which operates rams attached to the steering arms.

PAS assists the driver to turn. It only operates when the engine is running. If a fault develops you can retain control of the steering but a much greater effort is needed to turn the steering wheel. Movement at the steering wheel may also be felt as a series of jerks.

Safety

Do not attempt to drive a bus fitted with PAS

- without the engine running i.e. 'coasting'
- if the system is faulty

If a fault develops whilst travelling, stop as soon as you can safely do so and seek expert assistance.

Specialised Knowledge – taking care of your customers

Passengers with disabilities

'If someone smiles and takes the money with a little bit of patience, it makes the world of difference.'

'Just speaking carefully, looking at the person and giving them attention – not feeling rushed – matters a lot. The feeling that you're holding up a queue of people is a very anxiety – producing situation...'

These are comments from passengers about their local bus service. The sort of people you might carry every day. Regular customers, in fact. Yet each of them has a problem that may be hard to recognise.

Some disabilities are very obvious. A person carrying a white stick, or a long white cane, or accompanied by a guide dog is visually impaired. If the stick has red rings painted on it, they also have impaired hearing.

It is easy to see that someone with crutches, walking frames, or any other aid to movement, has a disability – perhaps only temporarily.

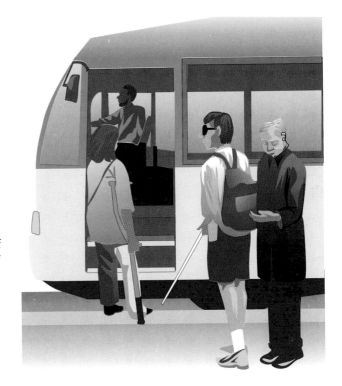

1

You may do specialised work helping people who, every day of their lives, face challenges to their mobility. You will be familiar with their problems.

If not, try to imagine what assistance you would like in their position. Try to be patient and considerate and always respect their wishes. Disabled people want to retain their independence. If someone tells you they can manage – let them. But be prepared to offer help if they appear to need it, or ask for it.

You will have your own problems to cope with – such as trying to keep to time; bad traffic conditions; inconsiderate behaviour by other road users – but you should do your best to offer courtesy and a smooth ride to those with special needs. Also, think about the everyday problems faced by people trying to manage with children, pushchairs or shopping trolleys.

Blind and partially sighted passengers

More than 200,000 people in the UK are visually impaired. Only a small proportion are totally blind, but you may not be able to tell by their appearance. Most partially sighted people find it hard to read a destination display or timetable. Visually handicapped people depend on their local bus service for mobility.

'There is a problem of explaining that we can't see very well ... we want to do as much as we can for ourselves and just be helped with the tiny bit that we can't do ...'

Deaf and hearing impaired passengers

'I usually ask the fare and if I don't hear how much it is, sometimes I bluff and just offer £1 and hope to get the right change. If the bus driver seems to be a pleasant, approachable person, I don't mind asking him to repeat it, but some drivers are under pressure and appear not to be aware of you or don't look at your face ...'

It is common courtesy to look at people when you speak to them. Just doing that will allow most deaf or hearing impaired people to understand you. Good communication saves time.

Passengers with physical disabilities

People with arthritis, stiff joints, artificial limbs or conditions such as multiple sclerosis often put up with extra pain (and the impatient reaction of other passengers) rather than ask for extra consideration on a bus. For them courtesy and a smooth ride are important.

A passenger suffering from arthritis made the point that:

'Nobody wants to shout to the rest of the world 'I am having trouble', but if the driver could just wait until you are sitting down before they pulled away...'

'If letting the clutch out or moving away is done too violently it hurts every inch of the way...'

'If the driver was to go round corners a little more slowly it would probably be less painful...'

1

Passengers with learning disabilities

Customers with learning disabilities may also appear fit and active, but they may find bus travel a special problem and challenge. It may be hard for them to understand other people or to make them understand you. Any unexpected problems can produce a sense of panic. People with learning disabilities are increasingly being encouraged to go out to work, to go shopping or visit friends. With patience and understanding you can contribute towards their confidence and sense of achievement.

Customer care

So, apart from offering a smile, a smooth ride and a lot of patience, what can you do to help every person in the bus queue?

Remember these points:

- be on the lookout. Waiting passengers may not be able to see or hear the bus coming

- eliminate the gap. Many passengers find it difficult to board and alight if the bus pulls up too far away from the kerb. Stop well in to help them

- look directly at each passenger when you speak. It may make a world of difference to some of your customers

- give less agile passengers time to get seated before you move off. A few seconds here will add very little to journey times but can make a huge difference to some customers.

Passenger lifts and ramps

Make sure you are thoroughly trained in the safe use of passenger lifts, ramps and securing devices if you drive a vehicle fitted with this equipment. Never let untrained people operate lifts and watch out for the safety of others at all times.

'Kneeling' buses

Some buses are equipped with air or hydraulic systems which allow the step level to be raised and lowered. This is helpful to ambulant disabled and elderly passengers. It is essential that you are thoroughly trained in the use of such systems and are aware of the principles of safe operation.

Environmental Issues

Vehicle designers, bus operators and maintenance staff all have a part in helping to reduce the effects that vehicles have on the environment. You can also help. You should be aware of the effects your vehicle, and the way in which it is driven and operated, can have on the environment around you.

The bus and coach industry has a major role in limiting the total number of vehicles on our roads. 1 double deck bus can carry the occupants of 20 cars. Only 1 engine needs to be running instead of 20. But a badly maintained or poorly driven vehicle can cause unnecessary pollution.

Make regular checks of your vehicle and ensure that any defects are reported and rectified, especially

- excessive exhaust smoke (the public is encouraged to report vehicles emitting excessive fumes)
- uneven running which may be caused by fuel pump or injector faults
- brake faults which can cause drag
- incorrect tyre pressures
- suspension system faults which may result in road surface damage.

Always drive with fuel economy in mind. Operators keep careful checks on vehicle running costs and fuel economy is a key factor for profitability, as well as reducing waste.

Aim to

- plan routes to avoid congestion
- anticipate well ahead
- avoid the need to 'make up time'
- avoid over revving (if a rev counter is fitted try to keep in the green band as much as possible)
- brake in good time (all braking wastes energy in the form of heat)
- where regenerative retarders are fitted make good use of them
- switch off your engine when stationary for some time, especially where noise and exhaust fumes cause annoyance
- allow air pressure to build up with the engine on tickover rather than 'revving up.'

1

Road friendly suspension

Many PCVs are fitted with air suspension to reduce wear on road surfaces.

Bumping over kerbs, verges and pavements damages them and underground services. Repair can be costly. You can also damage the vehicle's tyres and that may not be immediately obvious. Subsequent tyre failure may be catastrophic and you may not be the driver when it happens. But the responsibility will be yours.

Fuels

Take care to avoid spillages if you refuel your vehicle.

Diesel fuel is slippery and can be very dangerous for anyone stepping on to it (especially in garage areas). On the road it can create a serious risk to other road users; especially motorcyclists. It is a legal requirement that you check that all filler caps are properly closed and secure before driving off.

Diesel is the traditional fuel for PCV engines. However, a number of alternative fuels are being considered.

Compressed Natural Gas (CNG)

Although the quality of exhaust emissions produced has improved, there are technical problems with the size and design of the tanks required.

Methane and Hydrogen

Experiments are being carried out to assess whether these naturally occurring fuels could be used as alternatives to diesel.

Electricity

There have been trials with electric vehicles for a number of years, but it has so far proved difficult to solve the problems of battery size and capacity.

Audible warning systems

Some vehicles are fitted with a system which warns people that the vehicle is reversing.

Do not forget that

- bleepers
- horns
- voice warnings

must not be allowed to operate on a road subject to a 30 mph speed limit between 23.30 hrs and 07.00 hrs.

Also take care when setting vehicle alarm systems. There are restrictions on the length of time that the warning may sound. Environmental health officers are empowered to enter vehicles and disable the system if a nuisance is caused.

1

Legal Requirements

The number of people killed or injured on Britain's roads decreases every year. That is good news. Better driver education, better vehicle design and tougher legislation have helped improve driving standards and outlaw unsafe practices.

The laws covering PCVs and their drivers are extensive and sometimes complex, but their introduction has helped to give the industry a justifiably good safety record.

Although the passenger transport industry's safety record is good, there are still about 10,000 casualties in accidents involving buses and coaches every year. Most of the injuries sustained are not serious, but each year some 30 passengers are killed.

There is an average of more than 30 incidents involving PCVs every day. A small, but significant, proportion of those incidents involve a PCV driver breaking the law in some way.

Drivers are also prosecuted for offences where no accident has occurred.

Don't let it happen to you!

You must be sure that you comply with regulations which affect

- your conduct
- your health
- your safety
- your licence
- your hours of work
- your vehicle
- your driving
- your passengers.

Do not forget that ignorance is not accepted as a defence in law – even though the regulations concerned might only have changed the day before.

Your Conduct

Alcohol

It is an offence to drive with

- a breath alcohol level in excess of 35 microgrammes per 100 ml
- a blood alcohol level in excess of 80 mg per 100 ml.

If you are convicted of such an offence while driving a car, any driving ban will mean you also lose your PCV entitlement. That could mean you losing your job.

Do not drink and drive.

Alcohol may remain in the body's system for around 24 hours.

You could still fail a breath test the morning after drinking.

The only safe limit, ever, is a zero limit.

Drugs

Some operators, concerned about drug abuse amongst staff, have introduced random drug-testing for their drivers.

Drivers who fail such tests face instant dismissal.

It is obvious that you must not take any of the following drugs, classified as 'banned substances', whilst driving:

- Amphetamines e.g.'diet pills'
- Barbiturates (Sleeping pills)
- Benzodiazapine (Tranquillizers)
- Cannabis
- Cocaine
- Heroin
- Methaqualone (Sleeping pills)
- Methylamphetamines MDMA
- Morphine/codeine
- Phencyclidine ('Angel Dust')
- Propoxyphane.

Unlike alcohol, the effects of which last for about 24hrs, many of the effects of drugs remain in the body's system for up to 72 hrs.

Even everyday cold or 'flu remedies can cause drowsiness.

Read the label carefully!

If in doubt, consult either your doctor or pharmacist.

If still in doubt don't drive!

1

Health

Even apparently simple illnesses can affect your reactions.

You should be on your guard against the effects of

- a common cold
- 'flu symptoms
- hay fever
- tiredness and fatigue.

Health and Safety

A wide range of activities are the subject of Health and Safety regulations.

These include

- limits on the weight of objects which should be lifted manually (loading suitcases etc)

- requirements for protective clothing when handling oils and other maintenance materials and when disposing of waste (emptying toilet tanks etc)

- safe operating procedures in the event of emergencies or breakdowns

- safe working practices in garages, bus depots and bus stations.

Falling asleep

Previously unexplained incidents where vehicles have

- left the road
- collided with broken-down vehicles, police patrol officers or other people on the hard shoulders of motorways

have now been attributed to the problem of drivers falling asleep at the wheel.

When driving you may feel tired for reasons you may not appreciate.

Be on your guard against boredom on comparatively empty roads or motorways, especially at night.

Always

- take planned rest breaks
- keep a plentiful supply of fresh air circulating around the driving area
- avoid allowing the driving area to become too warm
- avoid driving if you are not 100% fit
- avoid driving after a heavy meal.

Being a professional means making sure you are fit for work. That includes making sure you get enough rest the night before an early start. You have to be capable of driving safely for the whole of your shift.

If you do start to feel tired or unable to concentrate, stop as soon as it is safe and legal to do so.

You may have to call out a relief driver if you are unable to continue or you are ill. It is much better to seek help rather than try and 'push on'. Try not to worry about inconveniencing your passengers or the company. It is better to arrive late than not at all.

Modern vehicles with air suspension, power steering and automatic transmission demand less of drivers than used to be the case. But modern road and traffic conditions continue to demand just as much concentration as ever. Most accidents occur as a result of a lapse in concentration.

Don't let one happen to you.

1 Safe working practices

Every year someone in the bus and coach industry is killed or badly injured in an incident involving moving vehicles in confined spaces. When parking close to the wall or another vehicle make sure

- you leave room for other vehicles
- you are not trapping or crushing anyone.

The bodies of vehicles fitted with air suspension may move a considerable amount when parked or when started, as air is exhausted or injected into the air bags. Parking one of these vehicles too close to a pillar, wall or another vehicle may cause damage or injury.

Vehicle maintenance and repair work is not normally your responsibility.

You should be able to recognise faults with your vehicle and fill in defect reports correctly. You may have to carry out minor emergency repairs on the road when conditions dictate. But don't attempt anything beyond that. You should not do any work on engines or any other vehicle components unless you are fully trained or supervised.

You should be careful of the following hazards in workshops and garages:

- asbestos dust
- paint spray
- solvents
- exhaust fumes
- degreasing agents
- inspection pits
- moving/reversing vehicles
- vehicle batteries
- vehicle chair lifts or 'kneeling' mechanisms
- bus washers.

If you don't have to be in the workshop or garage, don't.

The professional driving standards described in this book should also apply to drivers employed as 'shunters' or mechanics who drive buses and coaches as part of the job.

Your driving licence

You need your PCV licence in order to earn your living driving buses, coaches and minibuses. To keep it, you will want to drive to a high professional standard.

When you drive any other vehicle, your own car for example, it is essential that your driving continues to be to the same high standard.

Your PCV licence will be at risk if you accumulate penalty points from offences committed whilst driving any vehicle.

Speeding offences

A lot of police forces and local authorities now use up-to-date technology to persuade drivers to obey speed limits and to catch and prosecute those who don't.

Sophisticated detection equipment can `lock on' to individual vehicles in busy traffic flows. Cameras can photograph vehicles exceeding the speed limit.

At some motorway sites roadside detection equipment displays the registration number and speed of speeding vehicles to 'show-up' the drivers concerned.

Speeding drivers who have been prosecuted find that the penalties are often linked to how much the legal speed limit was exceeded.

The aim is to improve driving standards, not to increase prosecutions.

Your vehicle may be fitted with a speed limiter which will generally prevent you from exceeding set limits, but it won't stop you exceeding lower speed limits. Observing speed limits is part of your responsibility.

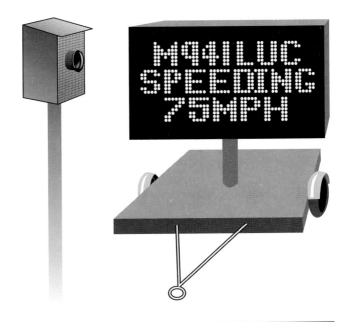

Red light cameras

Cameras are increasingly being installed at traffic light controlled junctions to record drivers not complying with the signals.

These are also intended to act as a deterrent and to improve safety for road users in general.

Any photograph produced as evidence which shows

- the time
- the date
- the speed
- the vehicle registration number
- the length of time a red signal had been showing

will prove difficult to dispute.

TIME: 1402
DATE: 27.02.94
SPEED: 32.7 MPH
NO. CAM: BD 37057

Legal Requirements

There are many Acts of Parliament, Statutory Instruments and EC Regulations which affect the bus and coach driver. It is not within the scope of this book to explain all the rules which apply. In general, this part of the chapter alerts you to legal aspects of driving PCVs which you must be aware of, even though they may not be your responsibility initially. Courts frequently find drivers guilty of offences when it would be reasonable to expect that they had checked that all was well, but had not done so.

If you are in any doubt about how regulations may affect your driving you should take legal advice.

Drivers' hours and records

Tachographs are needed under EC rules

- for all vehicles with more than 16 passenger seats except
  - those on regular services
  - some vehicles which are exempt
- for all vehicles with more than 8 passenger seats on EC international journeys.

There are regulations which require tachographs to be

- correctly calibrated before first use
- inspected every two years
- recalibrated after 6 years use.

The driver's hours rules are complex. Although there are exceptions, the basic requirements are

- the driver must carry enough charts of an approved type and which can be used in the instrument fitted to the vehicle for the whole journey
- dirty or damaged charts must not be used and the driver must fill in all the information detailed in the centre field of each chart before using it
- recordings must start as soon as the chart is placed in the instrument and the driver is responsible for the correct setting of the 'mode' switch at all times. This shows when the driver is
  - driving
  - carrying out other work
  - resting or taking a break.

Drivers must carry their record charts for at least the previous seven days and give them to their employer within twenty one days.

Employers must keep the charts for a specified time and produce them as required.

1

EC driving limits

You may drive for a maximum of 9 hours between any two rest periods (may be increased to 10 hours on two days in the week).

After 4 hours 30 minutes a break of 45 minutes must be taken. This may be replaced by other breaks of at least 15 minutes which occur either during, or during and after the 4 hours 30 minutes driving period, provided they add up to at least 45 minutes and you never exceed 4 hours 30 minutes continuous driving. It is generally accepted that a new driving period begins after 45 minutes total break time has been taken.

Minimum daily rest is 11 hours, although this may be reduced to 9 hours on three days of the week provided the reduction is 'made up' by the end of the following week.

There are exceptions which allow rest periods to be split or interrupted.

Maximum driving is six daily shifts in a week, not more than 90 hours in a fortnight and rest must normally be a minimum of 45 hours in each seven day period.

Special rules apply to two-man crews and when travelling on a ferry or train.

Regular services

A regular service on a route of over 50 km is subject to EC rules, but a tachograph is not needed as long as

- the employer draws up a service timetable and duty roster for crew members, records of which are kept for inspection

- the driver carries an extract from the duty roster and a copy of the service timetable.

A regular service on a route of up to 50km is free from the EC rules but will, in most cases, be subject to other rules.

Vehicles operating services under the 'permit' scheme may not require tachographs or be subject to the EC rules. This depends on the use made of the vehicle and the requirements will be explained when the permit is issued.

Legal Requirements

Speed Limiters

UK legislation

Since 1 April 1991 coaches which

• are over 7.5 tonnes

and

• are fitted with more than 16 passenger seats

and

• are capable of speeds over 70 mph

must be fitted with limiters set to 70 mph if first used on or after 1 April 1974 on national journeys.

Effects of EC Legislation

Since 1 January 1994 buses and coaches which

• are over 7.5 tonnes gross vehicle weight

and

• are capable of speeds over 65mph

must be fitted with a limiter set to 65 mph if first used on or after 1 January 1994 on national journeys.

Since 1 January 1995 buses and coaches which

• are over 7.5 tonnes gross vehicle weight

and

• are capable of speeds over 65mph

must be fitted with a limiter set to 65 mph if first used on or after 1 January 1988 on international journeys.

After 1 January 1996 buses and coaches which

• are over 7.5 tonnes gross vehicle weight

and

• are capable of speeds over 65mph

must also be fitted with a limiter set to 65 mph if first used on or after 1 January 1988 on national journeys.

The speed at which the limiter is set must be shown on a plate positioned in a conspicuous position in the driver's cab.

1 Legal Requirements

Your vehicle

The law relating to vehicles is extensive.

The manufacturer is responsible for ensuring that it is built to comply with construction and use regulations.

The operator is responsible for making sure

- that it continues to comply with those regulations

- that it meets all current requirements and all new regulations as they are introduced

- that it is tested as required

- that it displays all markings, discs and certificates required

- that all equipment, fittings and fixtures are in a serviceable condition

- that a system exists whereby drivers of the vehicle can report defects and have them rectified effectively

- that they do not cause or permit a vehicle to be operated in any way other than the law allows.

You are responsible for

- taking all reasonable precautions to ensure that all legal requirements are met before driving any vehicle

- checking that the vehicle is fully roadworthy and free from significant defects before driving it

- ensuring that any equipment, fittings or fixtures required are present and serviceable

- not driving the vehicle if any fault develops which would make it illegal to do so

- all actions you take whilst in charge of the vehicle being within the law.

The sensible approach to take requires you to consider if it would be illegal to drive the vehicle

- in service

- at all

if

- anything that should by law be fitted to or carried on the vehicle is

  - not in place

  - in an unserviceable or in a dangerous condition

  or

- something is fitted to the vehicle which is not required by law but is

  - unserviceable

  - in a dangerous condition

  - not fitted so as to comply with the regulations.*

* For example, your vehicle is not required by law to have spot or fog lights. However, if they are fitted they must be positioned according to the regulations and it is an offence if they do not work.

Legal Requirements

Your driving

When driving it is your responsibility to comply with all the regulations. You must keep up to date with road traffic rules and apply them.

This book covers the approach you should take as a professional PCV driver. It does not include general driving principles, that is everything you should know and apply when driving ANY vehicle.

You can refer to other books in this 'Driving Skills' series, such as 'Your Driving Test' and 'The Driving Manual' and you should refer to 'The Highway Code' regularly.

Books by other publishers also cover general driving rules and regulations.

Keep in mind that ignorance of the law is no defence and it is reasonable to expect that you, a professional driver, will be knowledgeable.

Your passengers

Various regulations cover how you deal with passengers and their behaviour.

Specific rules relate to

- the conduct of drivers, conductors, couriers and inspectors
- the number of passengers carried
- the carriage of schoolchildren
- the carriage and consumption of alcohol
- smoking
- passengers causing danger or offence by their
  - behaviour
  - condition
- the carriage or use of dangerous, noxious or illegal substances by passengers etc.

Company rules

In addition to the legal obligations and restrictions, most operators have specific rules which must be followed.

It is in your own interests to read them and comply with them.

You may risk dismissal if you fail to do so.

Anti theft measures

There are many anti theft systems on the market, some of which are being fitted to vehicles by manufacturers.

It is not intended to provide a detailed description of the precautions you can take to avoid having your vehicle stolen or broken into, except in general terms. To do so would alert criminals to ways in which they can be overcome.

Unless you are handing a vehicle over to another driver, or parking it on an operator's premises where it is safe to do so, do not

- leave a vehicle unlocked or unattended
- allow passengers to leave personal effects on board except in locked luggage lockers
- forget to set any fitted anti-theft devices.

THE HIGHWAY CODE

HMSO 99p NET

DEPARTMENT OF TRANSPORT

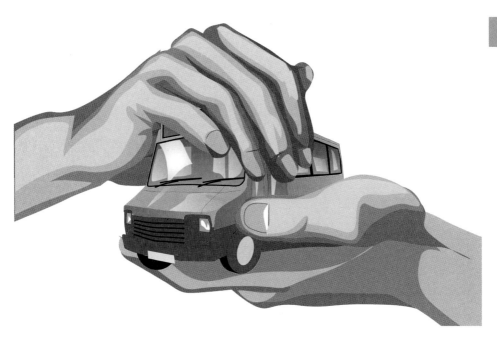

There are many different types of PCVs on the roads and each type requires different techniques to control it safely. Regular drivers will tell you that apparently identical buses have a different 'feel' to each of them. Professional drivers adapt their driving to suit the vehicle – they develop what is known as 'vehicle sympathy'.

In this book you will find sections which tell you to take corners slowly in order to keep your passengers comfortable. It is difficult to define what 'slowly' means for all vehicles on all occasions. A safe, comfortable speed will depend on how sharp the corner is and what other hazards there might be. The vehicle's design might dictate when the speed is comfortable. New coaches have very sophisticated air suspension levelling systems which allow relatively fast cornering whilst maintaining the body almost level. (If you drive a historic pre-1960 bus to rallies you will know that a tall, narrow body mounted on 'cart' springs can lean alarmingly even at walking pace). This chapter discusses some of the basic considerations, but it is up to you to develop your own 'vehicle sympathy' when driving.

1

Minibuses

A minibus is generally defined as a small bus seating between 9 and 16 passengers.

They are often based on van bodies and have been adapted by specialist firms, although some manufacturers produce purpose-built vehicles. The controls are usually similar to those on cars.

Drivers need only hold car licence entitlement (category B) to drive them for some uses. For other uses the driver needs category D1 entitlement (see page 222). Those vehicles operated under a community or minibus permit scheme are subject to special rules.

Few minibuses are built for full Public Service use, in which regulations require higher minimum standards for:

- headroom
- access
- seating
- safety precautions
- equipment
- markings.

You are strongly advised to seek professional training if you intend to drive minibuses. Various bodies run courses, but if you have difficulty finding one locally, contact RoSPA whose address and telephone number are on page 220.

Seat belts in minibuses

Seat belts save lives and reduce the risk of injury. Make sure you and your passengers are wearing seat belts where they are fitted.

All new minibuses must be equipped with belts. (The law may soon require that all buses used for the carriage of children must have them fitted.)

Some older minibuses may legally be used with only front seat driver and passenger belts. Most manufacturers will fit belts to earlier models and the cost of having this done is money well spent.

Minibuses are more likely to be driven by people who are not professional drivers.

Driving one is often a lot like driving a car, but you need to concentrate on the differences between the two types of vehicle.

Although minibuses might have power assisted steering and braking, and possibly an automatic gearbox, they can be more demanding and tiring than driving a car.

When driving a minibus think about

- Weight
  - greater stopping distances
  - slower to accelerate and to overtake
  - more effort needed for steering
- Height
  - greater body roll, pitch and sway
  - greater susceptibility to side winds etc.
- Noise levels
  - can be high, especially in van derived models
  - passenger noise can be high
- Speeds
  - more difficult to maintain high average speeds
  - speed may be lost rapidly on uphill stretches of road when fully laden
- The number of passengers
  - greater chance of distraction

- Time
  - plan your journey and estimate realistically how long it will take
  - allow plenty of time for the journey and put yourself under less pressure
  - take adequate breaks.

NEVER drive for more than 4½ hrs without taking a break of at least 45 minutes. This, and other rules, are legal requirements if you are subject to Drivers' Hours regulations.

- The distances travelled
  - is the vehicle suitable for long journeys?
  - would the use of a larger vehicle, possibly hired with a driver, be more appropriate?

Treat minibus driving as you would other work, even if it is not your normal job. You need to be alert and concentrate. Look at the rules in Chapter 7 which apply to professional drivers.

Consider carefully for each journey if

- you need someone else to drive
- a second driver to help you would be advisable.

Midibuses

There is no legal definition of a midibus. It is generally used to describe any single decker between a minibus and a 40+ seat coach or bus.

Virtually all are purpose built and many have bus or coach controls, equipment and other systems.

Depending on size, use and seating capacity, drivers require one of the following licence entitlements:

• category D

• category D1

• category D (restricted)

see pages 222 and 223.

Some midibuses operated under the community, minibus and large bus permit schemes can be driven with a category B (car) licence entitlement.

The rules are explained in booklet PSV 385 available from Traffic Area Offices.

Some midibuses are specialist vehicles with wheelchair lifts and securing equipment. Many are used on normal services where demand is not sufficient to justify the use of full size buses.

If used for the carriage of children, seat belts should be fitted. Seat belts should be worn by all passengers, if fitted.

It is essential that you fully understand the vehicle controls and, wherever possible, undergo 'type training.'

Many of the points mentioned earlier about minibuses also apply midibuses, as do many of the topics covered in the next two sections. In particular:

• blind spots and restricted vision

• standing passengers

• careful use of automatic gearboxes where fitted

• body roll.

Single deck service buses

These vehicles are generally designed for local bus service use and have basic passenger equipment. They may also have a limited amount of seating and a higher proportion of space for standing passengers. When used for school contract work they should have seat belts fitted and used. Most are one person operated.

Newer vehicles are built to the DIPTaC specification and may incorporate 'kneeling' suspension, wide doors and other design features to cater for customers with disabilities.

Because of the 'stop-start' nature of the journeys most of these vehicles have semi-automatic or fully automatic gearboxes, although some buses with manual gearboxes are still in use. All have relatively low gearing, with only four or five gears, or are coupled to low ratio drive axles to give greater flexibility at low speeds. As a result they may have lower top speeds.

All require skill and sensitivity to drive smoothly.

Coaches

Coaches are often downgraded to dual-purpose or service-bus use after several years of operation.

Some rural bus operators use coaches so their passengers travel in greater comfort. Lower specification running gear may be fitted to the vehicles to make it easier for the driver (less gear changing etc).

When vehicles are used for school contract work seat belts should be fitted and worn.

Coaches are designed to carry customers for longer distances, in greater comfort and with more facilities.

Most modern vehicles are high floor with rear or underfloor engines so that more luggage can be carried and to limit noise levels.

Many have sophisticated heating and air conditioning systems, toilets, catering areas and courier seats.

Coach journeys are longer and frequently use motorways, so manual gearboxes remain the norm, but they often have six or more gears, sometimes coupled with air assisted clutches or gear selection. Semi-automatic and fully automatic vehicles are in use and there is an increasing trend towards air suspension systems.

It is illegal for video and television screens to be visible to the driver or the occupants of other vehicles. It is essential, therefore, that curtains are fitted and closed when this equipment is in use.

Special regulations apply to the charging, use, location and emptying of water and toilet systems fitted to road vehicles.

See also pages 74 and 86.

Articulated ('bendi') buses

Articulated buses consist of a four wheel unit coupled to a two wheel rear section by means of floor and roof level pivots and a flexible shroud.

They offer high capacity urban transport in places where double deckers are impractical.

Trials have taken place in a number of towns in the UK with articulated buses, but there are relatively few in use.

They are more popular in other countries, particularly in Europe, where height limits of 4 metres exist.

In this country their length (up to 18 metres) can present problems when used on urban streets.

Great care is needed driving these vehicles. Always be aware of the 'swept path' the vehicle is taking.

When crossing road junctions and pulling into lay-bys allowances will have to be made for the length of the vehicle.

Do not obstruct other road users or get into a position which will require reversing the vehicle.

Unless special video reversing equipment is fitted, do not reverse unless an assistant stands outside at the back of the bus to help.

Licence requirements for these vehicles are explained on page 226.

'Type training' is essential before driving an articulated bus.

1

Light rail (or rapid) transit systems ('supertrams')

LRT systems are essentially modern tramways – the vehicles running singly or as multiple units on standard railway gauge track.

They are often completely segregated from other traffic and may run on former railway tracks.

The following points are important:

• in some towns and cities roads are restricted to buses and LRTs only

• where LRTs operate on roads not segregated from other traffic, drivers must hold full category B licence entitlement

• LRT drivers and vehicles are subject to all the normal rules of the road, in addition to specific rules about LRT operation

• other road users need to be aware of how to deal with LRTs and of their limitations.

LRT systems are common throughout Europe and are increasingly being introduced to cities in the UK. Drivers cannot operate 'supertrams' without extensive training.

All UK LRT and traditional tram operators have dedicated training schools and staff to ensure high safety standards.

LRT vehicles are fixed in the route they follow and cannot dodge around other vehicles and pedestrians.

The area occupied by an LRT vehicle is marked by paving or markings on the road surface. This 'swept path' must be kept clear at all times

Other road users, including bus and coach drivers, must avoid blocking 'supertram' routes.

When a tram approaches, other vehicles (and pedestrians) must

- keep away from the swept path area
- obey yellow box junction rules and not block junctions
- anticipate well ahead and NEVER stop on or across the tracks
- obey all traffic light signals and NEVER 'jump' lights which show the tram has priority.

Open top buses should not be driven beneath overhead LRT power supply lines.

Tram signs

Warning: trams on road

Speed limit for trams only

Trams travel in both directions. All other traffic obeys one way signs

Trams may proceed in direction shown on right whilst other traffic obeys traffic lights

Pedestrians; beware of trams

Lane for trams only

Trams only

Tram approaching when lights flash alternately

Double deck service buses

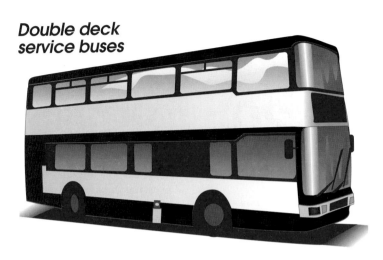

These are high capacity vehicles used primarily for stage carriage work.

Most are fitted with dual doors and fare collection equipment to allow for effective one person operation.

Extra internal mirrors are fitted to allow the driver to keep an eye on entrances, exits, stairs and the upper deck. To ensure high standards of passenger care and safety drivers should make full use of them.

Drivers need to balance safe driving with the comfort of passengers and the need to keep to timetables.

If used for school contract work, seat belts should be fitted and used. Seat belts should be worn by all passengers, if fitted.

Automatic and semi-automatic gearboxes are frequently fitted to these vehicles.

Make sure you know how to make smooth gearchanges and use the gearbox correctly when moving off and pulling up. Vehicle manufacturers give advice for each type of vehicle.

Smooth, skilful driving will be essential during peak periods when there will be more passengers standing, climbing the stairs and moving about the bus.

Most modern double deck vehicles have underfloor or rear mounted engines. You are less likely to know when the engine is overheating for example, so you will have to make full use of instruments

and warning lights to ensure early action should such a fault develop.

On double deck buses the driving position and front entrance are generally ahead of the front axle whilst the position of rear axles vary considerably. The wheelbase of the bus will dictate the appropriate course to take when cornering. This means that you must take care with overhangs and the danger of tyre damage on kerbs etc.

Read the information on vehicle height in chapter 5 and take extra care when driving open-top double deck buses.

Double deck coaches

The first double deck coaches were introduced in the UK in the 1950s. They were based on bus body shells but were fitted with more powerful engines and higher gearing. Coach seats were added to provide high capacity, luxury vehicles able to compete with other long distance passenger transport.

Since then there have been considerable developments, not least in the facilities double deck coaches now offer. Nearly all are now specially designed and purpose built. Comfort and customer service are the biggest selling points. Although some double deck coaches provide 70 or more seats, passenger carrying capacity is not always the key attraction to customers.

If used for school contract work, seat belts should be fitted and used. Seat belts should be worn by all passengers, if fitted.

These coaches may be fitted with

- toilets
- refreshment facilities
- lounges
- tables
- telephones and fax machines
- audio visual equipment
- crew sleeping accommodation.

On vehicles fitted with video and television equipment it is illegal for the screen to be visible to the driver or the occupants of other vehicles. It is essential, therefore, that curtains are fitted and closed when the equipment is in use.

Special regulations apply to the charging, use, location and emptying of water and toilet systems fitted to road vehicles.

See also pages 74 and 86.

A number of double deck coaches have a courier service and some specialist vehicles are designed to carry as few as twelve passengers with full sleeping or conference facilities provided.

These coaches are amongst the most sophisticated vehicles on the road with high output power units, versatile manual, automatic, semi-automatic or electronic gearboxes, air suspension and power assisted controls.

Make sure you understand all the systems fitted to the vehicle and are fully competent to operate them.

Driving positions may be unusual in these vehicles and

- the driver may not be able to see what is happening inside the coach
- video or electronic sensor systems may be fitted to help with manoeuvring and add to the view given by the rear-view mirrors
- additional mirrors may be fitted to show the driver what is happening below his field of vision at the front of the coach.

Use all these aids when driving to help you drive safely.

Six wheel double deckers

Higher vehicle weight has meant that air suspension is increasingly being fitted to all but the lightest PCVs to counter the damaging effects on roads and bridges.

Another recent development has been the addition of an extra rear axle to further distribute vehicle loads.

Popular in the 1930s before air suspension had been invented, few post-war vehicles were six wheelers, except for some coaches in the 1960s when an extra steering axle was added to the front.

In fact, the new generation of three axle buses and coaches may have 8 or 10 wheels – one or both of the rear axles carrying four.

Handling is not greatly different from two axle vehicles, except that punctures and blow outs are sometimes difficult to detect and frequent tyre checks are advised.

The course the wheels take on tight corners should be observed and allowed for when driving and very low speed when the steering is on full lock is advisable to minimise any possible 'scrubbing' effect on the rearmost tyres.

If used for school contract work, seat belts should be fitted and used. Seat belts should be worn by all passengers, if fitted.

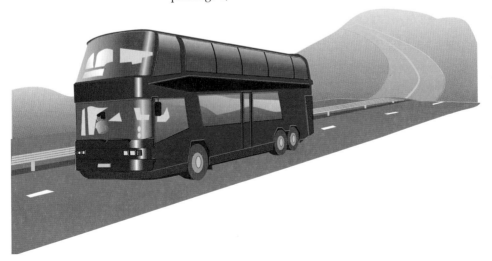

Historic buses and coaches

Enthusiasts have ensured that many historic buses and coaches have been preserved and are shown at rallies.

Some of these historic vehicles may be driven on a category B (car) licence entitlement, provided certain rules are observed.

These are

• the driver must be over 21

• the vehicle must carry less than 8 passengers.

Drivers with category D licence entitlements may drive historic buses and coaches as they would any other PCV.

If you intend to drive historic buses and coaches you should seek professional training.

For example, you need to know how to 'double-declutch' or 'snatch-change' to use crash or part-synchromesh gearboxes. These are special techniques which you should practise after they have been explained and demonstrated to you. Also, if the vehicle you drive has air or vacuum brakes, make sure that you understand the meaning of any warning signals.

Keeping historic vehicles in a roadworthy condition can be difficult and expensive. Repairs may be needed more often and spares may be difficult to obtain.

It is important that you never drive a preserved vehicle unless you are certain that it is fully roadworthy. Carry out all the checks in Chapter 7 and also make sure you are competent to drive the vehicle.

Older buses and coaches are more difficult to drive than modern counterparts. Engines, although often very large, delivered less power than nowadays. Generally, there was no power steering, air assisted clutches or semi-automatic gearboxes to make driving easier.

When driving these older vehicles:

• think how your slower speed affects other road users pull over to let them pass when you can do so safely

• treat the vehicle with respect

• ask for advice if you come across controls or warning systems that are unfamiliar

• make sure you have full control.

If you drive a vehicle for the first time start by mastering steering, gearchanging and braking techniques

• off the road

• under supervision

• without passengers.

Never

- drive a bus in which the driver has no contact with passengers without one designated responsible person in charge of the passenger saloon(s), unless

  - no passengers are carried

and

  - access to the vehicle is prevented by means of a door, chain, strap or other barrier

- allow passengers to ride on open platforms or with open doors

- allow more passengers to be carried than the vehicle is designed for, or the law allows

- allow bells to be used other than in the accepted way. In half-cab vehicles this is the only means of communication between the passenger saloon(s) and the driver.

Ensure that the bell codes are understood and that no-one else uses the bell except to give the 'stop' signal when necessary

The codes are:

1 bell – stop when safe

2 bells – move off when safe

3 bells – bus full

4 bells – emergency on bus.

Always take great care on rally sites when pedestrians are close to moving vehicles. Drive only at walking pace, or slower, and use marshalls or other responsible people to help you manoeuvre safely.

1

Mobile Project and playbuses

More than 500 double and single deck buses and coaches have been converted for community use in the UK.

As their primary purpose is for recreational, vocational or educational use they are not regarded as passenger carrying vehicles.

There are particular rules for their use and licensing requirements (see page 226). They may, in some cases, be driven by category B (car) licence holders.

The driving requirements for these large vehicles are the same whether an additional driving test has to be taken, or not. If you drive one of these vehicles it is essential that you are fully aware of your responsibilities.

Most are elderly buses which are 'life expired' for PCV operations. The importance of safety checks and adequate maintenance is greater as a result. Drivers must be able to identify faults and understand procedures for putting them right.

Be prepared

This book tells you what is expected of professional PCV drivers, but the advice applies to anyone who drives buses or coaches. A book cannot teach you to drive – you should always seek professional guidance before driving on public roads. You cannot expect to drive a bus, whatever its present use, without adequate training.

Operators and drivers of mobile project and play buses need to consider:

- safe stowage of equipment when the bus is being driven
- safe manoeuvring when arriving at, or departing from, sites
- safe installation and stowage of any heating, lighting or cooking equipment, including gas cylinders
- safe operation of generators and fuel storage.

Detailed guidance is available from the National Playbus Association whose address is on page 221.

Towing trailers

Considerable care is needed when towing trailers, especially when reversing. Extensive training and practice is strongly recommended.

Few buses and coaches in this country tow trailers. When they do, it is usually to provide additional luggage space.

Some mobile project and playbuses and some minibuses tow a trailer. This may contain a generator or other equipment.

Since 1 January 1993 the weight limit for single axle trailers hauled by holders of category D entitlement has been 5 tonnes.

From 1 July 1996 this will be further reduced to 750 kgs. From that date holders of category D entitlement will have to sit a D+E test to haul trailers over this weight.

Some articulated buses may require D+E entitlement. This depends on their construction.

This syllabus lists the skills and knowledge which you must have to be a bus or coach driver and to pass the PCV driving test. While training, use the syllabus as a check list. Make sure that you understand all the items. Other chapters of this book explain many topics in more detail. For some specialist information you will need to refer to other sources. Your local library will help. You can also ask your instructor for advice.

When you are on your driving test you will not be tested on all the items listed. You do need to understand them all, though. While you are driving your examiner will watch that you put your knowledge into practice and you will be asked questions. You will not know before the test which topics the questions will cover.

Think of passing the test as only one stage in becoming a good driver. You need to know about all aspects of being safe and professional.

If you drive a passenger carrying vehicle for which no special driving test is needed, the information contained in the syllabus will help you to achieve the high standard of driving required for your safety and that of your passengers.

1. Knowledge

A. You must have a thorough knowledge and understanding of

i the latest edition of The Highway Code, especially those sections which concern buses

ii regulations governing drivers' permitted hours (EC 3820/1985)

iii regulations relating to the carriage of passengers (Public Passenger Vehicles Act 1981 and 1990 amendments)

iv general motoring regulations, especially

- road traffic offences

- holding and producing driving licences

- holding operator's and road fund licences and displaying discs where applicable

- holding and displaying community bus permits where applicable

- insurance requirements (including 'green cards' or bail bonds that may be needed when abroad)

- the Temp 100 regulations if intending to drive outside the UK

- the information required to be shown on PCV manufacturer's plates

- annual testing and the certification requirements for tachographs and speed limiters

- the importance of regular vehicle maintenance and defect reporting procedures

v Health and Safety legislation as it applies to PCV duties.

B. You must also have a basic understanding of the function of the component parts of a PCV including

i internal combustion engines

- petrol
- diesel
- other fuels

ii power and control units in electrically propelled vehicles, if appropriate

iii ancillary and control systems

iv the body and its equipment.

Notes. Certain minibuses, mobile project buses, playbuses, historic vehicles and community buses are subject to a relaxation of the Public Service and Passenger Carrying Vehicle regulations.

If you drive one of these vehicles you must be aware of any restrictions as to its use.

If your vehicle is equipped with a trailer, you must know which legal requirements apply.

Note. This subject is covered in more detail in Section 3 of the syllabus.

2. Legal requirements

A. To learn to drive a PCV you must

i be 21 years old*

ii meet the stringent eyesight requirements

iii be medically fit to drive buses of any type

iv hold a full motor car licence (category B or, if issued prior to 1990, Group A)

v hold and comply with the conditions for holding either

  • a provisional PCV category D entitlement

  or

  • a full PCV entitlement for another category of vehicle which confers provisional entitlement for the vehicle you wish to drive

* Note. You may learn to drive a PCV and take the driving test between the ages of 18 and 21 but if you pass you are not permitted to carry passengers unless the vehicle is covered by a Public Service Vehicle operator's licence, bus or community bus permit and either

  • the bus has no more than 16 passenger seats and you drive only in the U.K.

  or

  • the route mileage does not exceed 50km (31 miles)

vi be sure that any vehicle driven

  • is legally roadworthy

  • has the required manufacturer's plate

  • has a current test certificate which covers its use

  • is properly licensed with the correct tax disc displayed (and 'O' licence or permit disc if required)

  • complies with the requirements of the tachograph and speed limiter legislation and displays the required certificates if applicable

  • meets minimum vehicle requirements if used for a PCV driving test

vii make sure the vehicle being driven is properly insured for its use, especially if it is on contract hire

viii display L-plates to the front and rear of the vehicle

ix be accompanied by a supervisor who holds a valid full UK licence for the category of vehicle

x be aware that it is a legal requirement to notify DVLA of any medical condition which could affect safe driving

xi ensure that all information required on the vehicle by law (referred to as the 'legal lettering') is displayed as applicable

  • seating/standing capacity

  • emergency exit location

  • fuel cut-off switch

  • electrical isolator switch

  • First Aid equipment

  • fire extinguisher

  • unladen weight of vehicle

  • height (must be displayed in the cab if the vehicle is over 3 metres (10 feet)

  • registered company name and address

  • engine stop button.

B. You must also avoid

i using any mobile telephone or radio transmitter whilst driving the vehicle (except for limited use of Band III radio systems used for route control and emergency purposes)

ii stopping on the hard shoulder of a motorway to use any mobile telephone or radio transmitter (unless in an emergency)

iii using any public address system fitted in the vehicle to give any commentary whilst driving (except for brief location information which may be given using a 'hands-off' system)

iv driving the vehicle whilst
- issuing tickets
- giving change
- holding a conversation other than in an emergency
- being distracted
- smoking
- any passenger doors are open.

C. You must know and apply the legal requirements relating to the vehicle and its use in respect of

i speed limits

ii seating/standing capacity

iii fire extinguishers

iv First Aid equipment (location and use)

v interior lighting during the hours of darkness

vi the carriage and consumption of alcoholic drinks

vii the emptying of toilet waste storage tanks

viii hazardous substances which may be brought on board by passengers

where applicable.

3. Vehicle controls, equipment and components

You must

i understand the function and use of the main controls of the vehicle
- accelerator
- clutch (see note)
- gears
- footbrake
- handbrake
- steering, including power assisted steering

and be able to use them competently

ii know the effects speed limiters will have on the control of your vehicle, especially when you intend to overtake

iii know the principles of the various systems of retarders which may be fitted to PCVs
- electric
- engine driven
- exhaust brakes

and when they should be brought into operation.

iv know the function of all other controls and switches on the vehicle and be able to use them competently

Note. Study those items which apply to your vehicle if it is fitted with automatic, or semi-automatic transmission.

v   understand the information given by

- gauges
- warning lights
- warning buzzer
- other displays on the instrument panel

vi be familiar with the operation of tachographs and their charts and any other time, speed or distance recording equipment which may be fitted. You should know what action to take if a fault develops in this equipment

vii know which checks should be made before starting a journey

viii know the safety factors relating to

- seated and standing passengers
- loading
- stability
- controls of any driver operated doors
- stowing luggage when passengers are carried

ix be able to carry out routine safety checks, and identify defects, especially with

- the engine
  - performance
  - fuel systems
  - lubricating systems and oil levels
  - coolant temperature and levels
  - exhaust systems
- the gearbox
  - operation
  - controls
- the transmission
- the braking system
  - efficiency
  - operation
- the steering (including power assisted systems)
- the suspension

- tyres and wheel security
- heating, air conditioning and ventilation
- electrical systems
  - lights
  - direction indicators
  - side and headlights
  - marker lights
  - fog and spot lights
  - reversing lights (and audible warnings if fitted)
  - brake lights
  - interior lights
  - step/entrance lights
  - destination displays
  - wipers and washers
  - bells and buzzers and linked 'bus stopping'displays
  - horns
  - fuses, cut-outs and relays

- bodywork
  - security and condition of exterior
  - panels
  - fittings
  - trim
  - access doors
  - rear view mirrors
  - of interior
  - seating
  - fittings
  - trim
  - floor coverings
  - mirrors

  and, where fitted,
  - seat belts
  - equipment for wheelchair access and security
  - mechanically, electrically or air operated doors
  - adjustable suspension on 'kneeling' vehicles
  - securing devices on emergency doors
  - emergency exit insecure warning device (light or buzzer)
  - equipment for breaking emergency windows
  - passenger grab rails
  - staircases.

4. Road user behaviour

You must know how to limit the risk of being involved in a road traffic accident by understanding

i   the most common causes of road traffic accidents

ii which road users are more vulnerable e.g
- children
- young riders and drivers
- elderly drivers
- elderly or infirm pedestrians
- cyclists and motorcyclists
- learner drivers

iii the rules, risks and effects of drinking before driving

iv the effects of
- illnesses
- drugs
- cold remedies
- other medication
- fatigue

on your performance

v   the importance of complying with rest period regulations

vi how to
- concentrate
- plan ahead
- anticipate the actions of other road users

5. Vehicle characteristics

A. You must know

i   the most important principles concerning braking distances under various

- road
- weather
- loading

conditions

ii the different handling characteristics of vehicles with regard to

- speed
- stability
- braking
- manoeuvrability
- turning circles

iii that some other vehicles, such as cycles and motorcycles, are less easily seen than others.

B. You must be aware of

i   the need to be extra vigilant when reversing any passenger carrying vehicle into or out of a bay

- at boarding points
- in workshops

ii the safe angle of tilt which must not be exceeded when driving high vehicles

iii the risks and difficulties presented when

- long vehicles negotiate speed reduction humps or hump-backed bridges
- high vehicles are driven along roads with an adverse camber and possible collision with
  - shop blinds
  - buildings
  - road signs
  - traffic lights
  - telephone poles
  - overhead cables
  - trees
  - lamp standards
  - scaffolding
  - other high vehicles
- vehicles with large mirrors pass close to
  - pedestrians
  - street 'furniture'
  - other vehicles
- heavy vehicles driving on, or close to, soft or damaged verges
- the height of the vehicle you are driving and the minimum clearance needed under bridges

v   the difficulties caused by the characteristics of both your own, and other, vehicles and be able to take the appropriate action to reduce any risks which may arise.

Examples of situations requiring special care are

- long wheelbase coaches, buses and large goods vehicles moving to the right before making a sharp left turn
- articulated vehicles having to take an unusual line before negotiating corners
  - roundabouts
  - entrances
- front and rear overhang on short wheelbase vehicles when turning left or right and at bus stops, lay-bys, pedestrian crossings etc.
- blind spots which occur on many large vehicles
- cycles, motorcycles and high-sided vehicles being buffeted in strong winds, especially on exposed sections of road
- turbulence created by coaches, double-decked buses and large goods vehicles travelling at speed affecting
  - pedestrians
  - cyclists
  - motorcyclists
  - vehicles towing caravans
  - smaller vehicles

Note. At all times remember that other road users may not understand the techniques required in order to manoeuvre a PCV safely.

1

6. Road and weather conditions

A. You must

i know about the hazards which can arise when driving on various types of road such as

- country lanes
- single track roads
- one-way streets
- those with bus lanes
- contra-flow systems
- streets in built-up areas
- three lane roads
- dual carriageways with various speed limits
- trunk roads with two-way traffic
- motorways
- roads or reserved areas where light rapid transit vehicles (supertrams) operate
- busways
- with differing volumes of traffic

- in various weather conditions such as
  - strong sunlight
  - rain
  - snow and ice
  - fog
  - wind (especially when driving high vehicles)
  - at all times of day and night*

ii know which surfaces will provide better or poorer grip when accelerating and braking

iii drive defensively and anticipate how the conditions may affect the driving of other road users

iv understand the need to be aware of other road users when pulling up at bus stops, especially near junctions

v appreciate the need to give correct signals especially before pulling up at
  - bus stops
  - close to a road junction
  - at pedestrian crossings etc.

vi recognise the special risks when
  - schoolchildren
  - elderly persons
  - disabled persons
  - passengers with
    - babies
    - toddlers
    - pushchairs
    - luggage

board or alight from your vehicle

vii be aware of the presence of other road users by making effective use of the mirrors and by looking round before moving off from standstill. Watch out, in particular, for the passenger who attempts to board or alight as you move off.

*Note. You should try to gain experience in as many of these situations as possible.

7. Traffic signs, rules and regulations

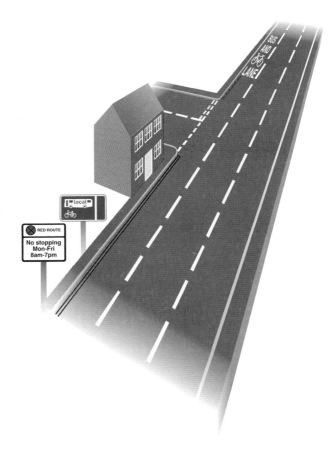

You must

i   have a thorough knowledge and understanding of the meanings of traffic signs and road markings, especially those relating to

- bus lanes (which, may also permit cycles and taxis)

- bus priority systems

- light rapid transit systems

ii   be able to recognise and comply with traffic signs such as

- weight limits

- height limits

- length limits

- width limits

- those prohibiting entry for motor vehicles

- no left or right turns

- loading/unloading restrictions

- roads designated Red Routes

- traffic calming measures.

Note. Some signs may exempt buses.

1

8. Vehicle control and road procedure

You must have the knowledge and skill to take the following precautions, some of which will require assistance

i Before getting into the vehicle check

- that you have all the required paperwork (especially for foreign trips)
- that all required discs and certificates are displayed
- all round for obstructions
- that the emergency exit(s) operate correctly and is (are) closed securely
- that all bulbs, lenses and reflectors are fitted, clean and undamaged
- that all lights, including indicators and stop lights, are undamaged and working
- tyres and wheelnuts for obvious defects (visual check)
- that all windows and mirrors are clean and free of traffic grime and cracks
- that all body panels are secure

- that all external lockers and crew compartment doors are secure
- that there are no fluid or air system leaks
- that fuel and electrical isolation switches are clearly marked and turned on
- that all route numbers and destination blinds or displays are correct (or replaced by information that the vehicle is not in service).

ii After entering the vehicle check

- the correct operation of any warning device fitted to an emergency exit which is not visible from the driving position
- that the entrance and exit doors (if fitted) operate correctly and that any warning systems work properly
- the location of the fire extinguisher(s) and First Aid equipment
- that heating, air conditioning or ventilation equipment is working properly and set for the conditions

Note. Controls for route and destination displays are usually on board the vehicle. Adjust them as necessary.

- that the bell or buzzer signal and any passenger information system works
- that all gangways and staircases are clean, clear and free from defects
- that all seats are clean, secure and free from defects
- that the interior lighting operates correctly including the exit/entrance step lights
- that equipment for wheelchair access is operational

where these items are fitted.

Make sure

- that the interior is acceptably clean
- that any graffiti is removed at the earliest opportunity, especially if it may cause offence
- that any luggage or equipment is safely stowed.

iii Before starting the engine check

- that the handbrake is applied and the gear selector is in neutral or the 'start' position.
- your seat, if necessary, for
  - height
  - distance from the controls
  - support and comfort
  - maximum vision
- the mirrors, if necessary, to give a clear view of
  - traffic behind
  - the entrance/exit
  - intending passengers
  - the upper deck (where appropriate)
- the doors (if fitted) are closed
- seat belts (if fitted) are in use

iv When you start the engine, but before moving, off check

- that the vehicle lights are on, if required
- that gauges indicate correct pressures for braking and ancillary systems
- that no warning lights are showing that indicate it is unsafe to drive the vehicle

- that no warning buzzer is operating
- that all fuel and temperature gauges are operating normally and that there is sufficient fuel for your journey
- that suspension systems are at the correct height, if appropriate
- that all doors are closed
- that all equipment operates correctly (wipers, washers, indicators etc.)
- that special access facilities, such as kneeling suspension, ramps or lifts are correctly adjusted or stowed
- that it is safe, by looking all round. Before moving off especially check
  - the blind spots
  - entry/exit door(s) or boarding platform(s)

near the wheels.

Note. Be aware that air operated systems, such as suspension and doors, may come into operation as air pressure builds up. Ensure this happens safely.

v At the first opportunity and BEFORE carrying passengers check

- brakes
- steering

for correct and effective operation

- that exhaust emissions are not excessive (when the engine is warm).

vi When driving you must be able to

- move off safely
  - straight ahead
  - at an angle
  - on the level
  - uphill
  - downhill
- select the correct road position and appropriate gear at all times
- take effective observation in all traffic conditions and give appropriate signals when necessary
- drive at a speed appropriate to the road, traffic and weather conditions
- anticipate changes in traffic conditions
- take the correct action at all times and exercise vehicle sympathy

1

- move into the appropriate traffic lane correctly and in good time
- pass stationary vehicles safely
- meet, overtake and cross the path of other vehicles safely
- turn right or left, or drive ahead at
  - junctions
  - crossroads
  - roundabouts
- keep a safe separation gap when following other vehicles
- act correctly at all types of pedestrian crossing
- show proper regard for the safety of all other road users, with particular respect for those most vulnerable
- keep up with the flow of traffic where it is safe and appropriate to do so, whilst observing all speed limits

- comply with
  - traffic regulations
  - traffic signs
  - signals given by authorised persons
  - police officers
  - traffic wardens
  - school crossing patrols
- take the correct action on signals given by other road users
- stop the vehicle safely at all times
- show courtesy and consideration to passengers at all times, particularly those with special needs
- wait until elderly or disabled passengers are seated
- be aware at all times of the effects that harsh
  - braking
  - acceleration
  - steering

will have on passengers, especially those

  - standing
  - moving toward exits
  - moving away from entrances

and pay particular attention to the care of

  - the elderly
  - the disabled
  - mothers with babies or toddlers

- cross all types of level crossings
  - railway
  - light rapid or railed transit systems (LRTs or 'supertrams')

where appropriate select safe and suitable places to stop the vehicle as close to the nearside kerb as is safe and practicable when requested

  - on the level
  - facing uphill
  - facing downhill
  - before reaching a parked vehicle
- leaving sufficient room to move away
  - with the platform of the vehicle close to passenger boarding points at bus stops and when requested on 'hail and ride' services.
- stop the vehicle in an emergency
  - safely
  - as quickly as possible
  - under full control
  - within a reasonable distance

- reverse the vehicle
  - under control
  - with effective observation
  - accurately
- to enter a restricted opening to the left or right
  - to stop with the extreme rear of the vehicle where required
- adhere to advertised timetables and, in particular, not depart early from published timing points.

Notes. You must be able to carry out all these checks and manoeuvres

- safely and expertly
- in daylight
- during the hours of darkness

as necessary.

Where your actions may affect other road users you must

- make proper use of the mirrors
- take effective observation
- give signals, when necessary
- act predictably

For the PCV driving test you will be asked to carry out specific exercises to demonstrate your ability to stop quickly and to reverse. If the test is not conducted by a Driving Standards Agency examiner, but by a delegated (company) examiner, these manoeuvres may be carried out on public roads.

vii Before leaving the driver's position you must make sure that

- the vehicle is stopped in a safe, legal and secure place
- the handbrake is on
- the gear lever/selector is in neutral or 'park'
- the engine is stopped
- the keys have been removed from the starter switch (if applicable)
- the electrical system is switched off unless lights or other systems are required (On some vehicles the switch may not be within reach of the driving position)
- you will not endanger anyone when you open any door.

viii When leaving a vehicle make sure that

1

- all windows are closed
- the passenger door is secure (if fitted)
- you take all possible precautions to prevent theft of the vehicle
- any available anti-theft device is used (e.g.immobilizer/alarm)
- you have selected a safe place to leave the unattended vehicle.
- the parking place is
  - legal (not a no waiting zone)
  - safe (will not endanger any member of the public)
  - convenient (not blocking any access or exit)
  - suitable (level and firm enough to support the weight of the vehicle)
  - not likely to create an unnecessary hazard for other road users.

ix If you will be leaving the vehicle but the public will still have access (for instance on playbuses or mobile project vehicles) ensure

- that the cab area is isolated
- that a responsible person is in attendance.

9. Additional knowledge

A. You must know

i the importance of inspecting all tyres on the vehicle for

- correct pressure
- signs of wear
- evidence of damage
- safe tread depth
- objects between twin tyres
- indications of overheating

ii safe driving principles which will help to prevent skids occurring and the action to take if they do

iii how to drive when the road is

- icy or snow-covered
- flooded
- covered by excess surface water, loose chippings or spillages

iv what to do if you are involved in a road traffic accident

- not resulting in injury (damage only)
- resulting in injury or involving fire
- where there is spillage of hazardous material
- where danger to other road users results from obstruction caused by an immobilized vehicle
- on a motorway

v the action to take if your vehicle breaks down

- in the day time
- at night

on

- a bend
- a road with two-way traffic
- a busy dual carriageway
- a clearway
- a motorway
- a railway or LRT crossing

with particular reference to the safety of passengers

vi the correct procedure to adopt if an accident occurs which involves a passenger

- travelling on your vehicle (falling etc.)
- boarding or alighting

vii the dimensions of your vehicle including the correct height – especially that of double-decked vehicles in respect of dangers presented by low bridges etc

viii the weight of your vehicle in respect of restrictions on weak bridges etc

ix the correct procedure to adopt if it becomes necessary to reverse the vehicle while carrying passengers

x the differences between toughened and laminated glass used in windows and windscreens

xi how to use the hammer or similar tool, if required, to exit from the vehicle in an emergency

xii basic First Aid for use on the road

xiii the correct legal procedure (defined in the 1990 amendments to the 1981 PSV regulations) to be adopted by the driver or, where present, a conductor or courier, in respect of any passenger(s) whose behaviour or condition affects

- the safety of other passengers
- the comfort of other passengers
- the safety of the crew

xiv the appropriate action to take when handed or when finding

- any lost property
- suspicious packages

xv the correct action to take in the event of a passenger or intending passenger attempting to alight from, or board, a moving vehicle

xvi how and when to use fire extinguishers fitted to the vehicle

xvii how to evacuate a PCV when necessary

xviii how and when to use emergency radio and public address systems, if fitted.

B. You must appreciate

i   the importance of avoiding any action which could cause offence or provoke physical retaliation

ii the need to keep control of the permitted number of standing passengers – especially at peak travel times

iii the need to use safe driving techniques and to obey all speed limits when attempting to maintain schedules laid down in the operator's timetable

iv the principles of passenger care including

- how to communicate effectively

- how to assist passengers with special needs

- how to help passengers unfamiliar with the service

v   the importance of presenting a positive image of your company and the industry through your appearance, conduct and condition of your vehicle.

C. You must be able to

i   make a written report promptly detailing any defects or symptoms of defects that could adversely affect the safe operation of vehicles and submit it to the designated person

(The recommended system requires a daily 'nil' return to be made to ensure that checks are made)

ii appreciate when defects are serious enough to require an unroadworthy vehicle to be removed from service

iii judge whether a defect is serious enough to cause a vehicle to be unsafe to be driven at all.

10. Motorway driving

1

You must have a thorough practical knowledge of the special

- rules

- regulations

- driving techniques

which apply to motorways.

You will not be asked to drive on the motorway on your PCV driving test. You will be expected to show a thorough understanding and knowledge of all aspects of motorway driving.

In particular

- overtaking

- exercising lane discipline

- when lanes are prohibited to certain PCVs

- when speed limiters affect driving

- where PCV speed limits differ to those applying to other traffic

- where temporary speed limits apply

- joining and leaving motorways

- breakdowns and emergencies

- driving in all weather conditions

- the principal causes of accidents on motorways.

1

11. Safe working practices

i   Avoid the risks involved in jumping down from cabs (where applicable)

ii Ensure any door in the driver's cab (as well as any passenger door) is properly closed while the vehicle is being driven

iii Follow safety guidelines when operating
- under
  - raised engine cowlings
  - raised luggage compartment hatches
  - overhead cables
  - any vehicle
- near
  - inspection pits
  - wheelchair lift controls
  - refuelling points
  - parked vehicles (especially those likely to be moved or with air suspension)
- whilst
  - carrying out roadside repairs
  - inflating tyres
  - near any vehicle supported on jacks
  - refuelling
  - topping up oil or water

iv Wear protective clothing, including gloves, when
- refuelling
- topping up oil or water
- checking battery levels
- emptying waste systems

v   Where company policy permits the driver to carry out minor repairs, do so only
- if you fully understand how to locate the fault and are able to put it right properly
- if you can do so without endangering yourself or others
- with the aid of appropriate equipment if it is needed
- if you are sure that any work you do will not invalidate any manufacturer's warranty

If in doubt, refer to your company.

New Legislation

From 1 April 1995 buses carrying children must display a distinctive yellow reflective sign on the front and rear, unless running a scheduled service for use by the general public.

Buses displaying the sign are permitted to use hazard warning lights when stationary and children are boarding or alighting.

In July 1994 the Secretary of State for Transport announced that the UK was to seek agreement to act ahead of the EU to introduce the compulsory fitment and use of seat belts in all minibuses and coaches used specifically for the transport of children.

It was also announced that the existing concession which allows 3 children to occupy 2 seats was to end.

At the time of going to press the legislation was not in place for these measures. However these and other changes to the law are imminent and PCV drivers must be aware of developments.

This part of the book is about the PCV driving test.

Chapter 8 outlines how to prepare for the test and what to expect when you take it. It explains how to apply for the test and what you should do if there are special circumstances.

Chapter 9 describes the test in detail.

The standard required to pass the PCV driving test has to be high. The vehicles you will be licensed to drive require extensive knowledge, skill and responsibility to be driven safely.

The driving test has been carefully designed to assess whether you have reached that required standard. If you are properly prepared, cover the officially recommended syllabus and combine this with practice on a wide variety of roads in different traffic conditions, you should be able to demonstrate to the examiner that you can deal with any situation that arises safely and skilfully without help or advice.

Choosing a Training Organisation

2

There is no DSA Register of Approved Instructors who teach pupils how to drive a bus, coach or minibus, as there is when learning to drive a motor car.

However, there are a number of training organisations concerned with passenger transport who have established the highest standards of training for the PCV licence.

Several large operators have driver training divisions. If you wish to work for one of them and are accepted onto the scheme they operate, you will be trained to drive using company buses.

You may have to pay for this training, or agree to work for the company for a certain time.

The company will arrange for your PCV driving test if you are good enough. Some operators have examiners of their own who are authorised to conduct tests. Otherwise you will be tested by a DSA examiner at a PCV driving test centre.

You can find details of a local training group by contacting the Confederation of Passenger Transport UK whose address is given on page 220 of this book; by approaching your local bus or coach operators; by contacting your local Training and Enterprise Council (TEC); or from advertisements or entries in your local press or trade directories.

You will normally be offered an 'assessment drive' lasting an hour or two. The instructor will then suggest the length of course you will need and the cost.

Contact more than one training organisation, and compare schemes. Talk to newly qualified PCV drivers about their training, if you can.

Try to choose an instructor or organisation with an established reputation for quality of instruction and proven PCV test results.

Ask what arrangements are made should you need additional training as a result of failing a PCV test.

Training can be costly, but high quality training is a good investment for your future. Try to choose carefully.

It is in your own interests to find out how comprehensive the course will be before you enrol.

Obviously the opportunity to drive a variety of vehicles will widen your knowledge and understanding of buses and coaches.

Practice

Your training should cover driving

- on as many different types of road as possible
- in all sorts of traffic conditions, including darkness
- on dual carriageways where the upper speed limit for PCVs applies.

You will probably be asked to drive on such roads during the PCV test.

Motorways

Although PCV learner drivers are permitted to drive on motorways you will not be expected to do so on the PCV driving test.

It is in your interests to gain experience of motorway driving while still under supervision.

You will be expected to answer questions which are intended to demonstrate that you have a **thorough** understanding of motorway rules – and, in particular, those which affect PCV drivers.

Practising Manoeuvres

You should have the opportunity to practise the braking and the reversing exercises on a suitable off-road site.

Avoid concentrating solely on them.

What to avoid when you practise

• creating undue inconvenience for others.

Not all road users appreciate the difficulties which a bus driver faces when manoeuvring a large vehicle, especially

– moving off

– stopping

– turning left or right

– in narrow roads

• causing nuisance to residents and other traffic.

The continuous noise created by

– the hissing of air brakes

– revving the engine to build-up air pressure

– persistent stopping and starting

can soon become a reason for complaint in residential areas.

If a local problem already exists due to PCV or LGV training taking place, avoid making the situation worse. Your trainer should be aware of any such difficulties and use an alternative area to practise.

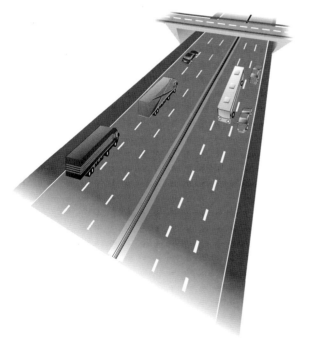

Part 2 The Passenger Carrying Vehicle Driving Test

Covering the syllabus

2

Whether you select operator training, a commercial driver training school or an individual trainer, with perhaps only one vehicle, it is essential that all aspects of the syllabus set out in Section 7 are covered.

About the PCV driving test

You should aim for a professional standard.

You will pass if the examiner sees that you can

- drive safely to a high standard
- show expert handling of all controls
- carry out the set exercises accurately and under control
- show a thorough knowledge of The Highway Code and vehicle safety matters.

Uniform standards

Examiners are trained to carry out tests to the same high standards nationally.

Whether DSA examiners or delegated company examiners, all are regularly checked to ensure that your driving will be assessed uniformly. You should have the same result whoever the examiner is and wherever the test takes place.

Test routes

- are as similar as possible
- include a wide range of typical road and traffic conditions.

Passengers

A DSA supervising officer (and sometimes other DSA staff) may sit in on your test. Do not let this worry you. The supervising officer will not be examining you, but making sure the examiner is carrying out the test properly.

Since the supervising officer will not interfere with the test or the result, just carry on as if he (or she) was not there.

Presence of trainers during the test

Your instructor or accompanying driver is allowed to be present during the test, but must not take any part in it.

Interpreters

If you need an interpreter you should arrange for one to come with you on the test. You should discuss with the examiner (through your interpreter) how you can both ensure that directions, questions and answers can be clearly understood.

The regulations do not permit other passengers to be carried on a driving test.

What the examiner expects

The examiner will want to see you drive safely to a high standard under various road and traffic conditions.

He (or she) will

• ask you questions

• give you directions clearly and in good time

• ask you to carry out set exercises.

The examiner will be understanding and sympathetic, and will make every effort to allow you to do your best.

Listen carefully to what is said. Examiners appreciate that there may be a higher noise level in some vehicles, and will make sure that you can hear any instructions or directions clearly.

If you do not hear or understand something do not be afraid to say so. The examiner will not mind.

If you are asked a question try to

• think about what has been asked before answering. (In driving terms this is known as making sure that you engage your brain before releasing your mouth).

• answer briefly but completely

• if you really don't know the answer, say so.

Don't waste time by waffling.

To avoid distracting you, the examiner will not engage you in any unnecessary conversation while you are busy driving.

He or she may talk to you whilst you are not driving, just to put you at your ease.

There are no trick questions– most examiners are genuinely interested in the people they meet and the work that they do.

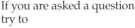

2

Your performance

Drive in the way your instructor has taught you. If you make a mistake, try not to worry. It may not be serious enough to affect the result of the test.

The examiner will be looking for an overall high standard and you are unlikely to fail for one or two minor mistakes.

The PCV driving test

The test will last around 1½ hours.

Apart from general driving, which will be described in more detail in Chapter 9, the test will include

• special exercises

  – reversing within a marked area into a restricted opening

  – a braking exercise

  – a gear changing exercise

  – moving off on the level, at an angle, uphill, and downhill

• questions on

  – *The Highway Code*

  – other matters relating to safe operation and driving.

These are usually asked at the end of the PCV driving test.

Special Exercises

Two of the special exercises are carried out on site at the PCV driving test centre.

If a delegated company examiner conducts your test they may be carried out on public roads or on an agreed private site.

These are

- the reversing exercise
- the braking exercise

The remainder of the special exercises will take place during the road section of the test.

The examiner will be as helpful as possible, and will explain what is required by showing you a diagram of the exercises and then asking you to carry them out.

If you are unsure about anything, ask!

The examiner will explain again.

During the reversing exercise, the examiner will remain outside the vehicle.

However, the examiner will join you in the cab before explaining the braking exercise to you and will watch your handling of the controls when you carry out the exercise.

Make sure you understand what is required!

The braking exercise is *always* carried out before leaving the PCV driving test centre.

If your vehicle does not pull up satisfactorily, the examiner may decide not to continue the test in the interests of safety.

The Highway Code

2

You must

- know and understand *The Highway Code* **thoroughly**
- obey it during the test
- answer questions on it.

So study the latest edition carefully!

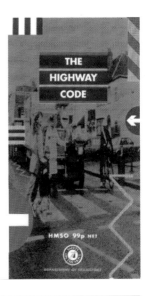

Part 2 The Passenger Carrying Vehicle Driving Test

Form DLV26 CC

DLV 26 CC
(10/94)

DSA DRIVING STANDARDS AGENCY

Application for a Large Goods Vehicle (LGV) or Passenger Carrying Vehicle (PCV) Driving Test Appointment

Please read the notes overleaf before completing this form.

Please do not write in this box

1 Ordinary Driving Licence Details

Driver No

Type of Test (please tick one box)
Large goods vehicle ☐   Passenger carrying vehicle ☐

Vocational Licence Held (please tick)

LGV ☐   Provisional ☐   Full ☐

PCV ☐   Provisional ☐   Full ☐

Expiry Date

Categories held

2 Personal Details

Surname

First name and Initial(s)

Address

Postcode

☎ Home   Work

3 Details of Test Appointment

Choice of Centre

Training Group Code

Earliest Date you will be available for test
Day   Month   Year

• Saturday Test ☐   • Weekday evening Test (summer only) ☐

(please tick box if applicable)

Unacceptable Days (Please tick any days you are unavailable)

	Mon		Tue		Wed		Thur		Fri		Sat	
	am	pm	am	pm	am	pm	am	pm	am	pm	am	pm
	1	2	3	4	5	6	7	8	9	10		

Unacceptable Dates (Please enter details)

Are there any special circumstances (such as a disibility that might affect your driving). Please give details.

4 Test Vehicle Details

Overall Dimensions (metres) (please complete in all cases)
Length   Height   Width

Large Goods Vehicles (please tick category)   Man Auto

		Man	Auto
Goods vehicles over 7.5 tonnes	C		
Articulated goods vehicles over 7.5 tonnes	C+E		
Goods vehicle and trailer combination of at least 15 tonnes gross	C+E		

Cab Seating Capacity

Passenger Carrying Vehicles   Man Auto

		Man	Auto
PCV with 9 passenger seats or more, 9 metres or more in length, and capable of 80kph/50mph	D		
PCV with 9 passenger seats or more, **less** than 9 metres in length, and capable of 80kph/50mph	D (fewer than 17 passenger seats		
PCV with 9 passenger seats or more, 9 metres or more in length, with a trailer over 1250kgs, and capable of 80kph/50mph	D+E		

Important: See notes overleaf

5   Fee enclosed   Cheque/postal order No.

£

Signed

Date

£

I wish to pay by Visa/MasterCard/Delta. Please charge to my account. My card number is (13 or 16 digits)

VISA   Signature of card holder   Expiry date

MasterCard.   Name of card holder

DELTA   Address of card holder

Postcode

Applying for the PCV Driving Test

You must already have entitlement to drive PCVs (either a category D provisional licence, or a full licence for a category which includes provisional entitlement for the category you wish to be tested on) before applying for the test.

Apply in good time, but only when you are sure your driving has reached the standards set out in this book.

You should ensure that you receive first class instruction – together with as much practice as possible.

Only when you are driving

• consistently well

• with confidence

• in complete control

• without assistance and guidance from your instructor

will you be really ready for your PCV driving test.

Those who fail the test often do so because they have not had enough instruction and practice.

Special circumstances

To make sure that enough time is allowed for your test, it would help the DSA to know

• if you are restricted in any way in your movements

• if you have any disability which may affect your driving

• if you will need to use an interpreter.

So, if any of these apply to you, please include this information on your test application form.

Drivers with Disabilities

Whatever the nature of your disability, you will still take the same PCV driving test as every other candidate.

Your examiner may wish to talk to you about your disability and any adaptations fitted to your vehicle.

For this reason, it is important to give details of your disability when you apply for your test.

If you would like further information, please see the list of useful addresses at the back of this book.

2

2

Saturday tests

Saturday tests are available at some PCV Driving Test Centres. The fees are higher than for a test during normal working hours on weekdays.You can get details from

- DSA Regional Offices
- PCV Driving Test Centres.

Extended Tests

If you are found guilty of certain driving offences, the Courts may direct you to retake your PCV driving test. For some offences which involve disqualification from driving for a period of time, the Courts must direct you to take an extended car driving test.

- it may then necessary for you to pass a normal PCV driving test if you previously held a PCV entitlement and wish to regain it
- you may only apply for a PCV test after passing an extended category B driving test
- it will be necessary to apply to DVLC for a provisional licence entitlement.

There is a higher fee for the extended car driving test.

Application Form

You can obtain an application form (DLV 26) for the driving test from any DSA Regional Office. (See list of addresses at the back of this book.)

Study the guidance notes carefully, including the table of passenger carrying vehicle categories, especially if you wish to drive more than one category. Note that, should you pass the test on a semi- or fully automatic vehicle, you will not be able to drive buses with a manual gearbox.

Make sure you give all the particulars asked for on the application form otherwise the form will only have to be returned to you, and your driving test appointment will be delayed.

Send the correct fee with your application.

Posters at test centres list the fees, or your DSA Regional Office will tell you.

- Cheques

or

- Postal Orders

should be crossed and made payable to 'Driving Standards Agency' **Do not send cash.**

If you send a Postal Order, keep the counterfoil.

Send your application to DSA at least 28 days before your preferred date for test (in summer, longer notice is often helpful due to increased demand). Programmes of tests are arranged well in advance and, if you do not give enough notice, you may not be given your preferred date.

Send your application to the appropriate DSA Regional Office making sure that you

- address your application correctly
- enclose the correct fee

otherwise your application will be delayed.

Credit and Debit card applications

You can book your PCV driving test by telephone using a credit card. If the card is not yours, its holder should be with you when you make the call.

The following are accepted

• Mastercard

• Visa

• Delta

The telephone number is on page 217, listed under the DSA Regional Office responsible for the centre you wish to use for the test.

You will find it helpful to have filled in an application form (DLV26 or DLV26CC) before making the call. You will be asked for the information listed on the form.

Trainer bookings

DSA has an arrangement with some trainers for them to book tests for candidates.

At the time of writing these arrangements are being changed.

Ask at the training school whether you are able to take advantage of the scheme or if you should book the test for yourself.

If you take the test with a delegated examiner from an operator's premises, the test will usually be offered to you at the end of the course. The cost will normally be included as part of your agreement with the company, but you may be asked to pay a separate fee.

Trainers wishing to use the trainer booking system should contact the DSA Regional Office for their area.

Being prepared for the test

2

When you learned to drive a car, it is likely that you waited until you were advised that you were ready for a test before you applied.

Driver training for buses, coaches and lorries is usually intensive. It may be necessary for you or your trainer to book your PCV test before you have reached the standard of driving required to pass.

Having a test date to aim for is a good incentive. However, drivers acquire skills and understanding at differing rates and it is possible that you may need more time and training than you had planned.

If so, do not be afraid to postpone your test. Be advised by your trainer. A late cancellation may result in you losing your fee for the driving test, but you must consider this against the risk you run if you drive unaccompanied on your test when you are not competent.

Driving examiners are observers during a driving test. They are not there to advise you how to drive. The nature of their work means that they will probably not be in a position to intervene if you make a serious or dangerous mistake.

If your instructor does not feel that you have competent, safe control of the vehicle by the time of the test appointment, accept that judgement. You will be advised about the options for additional training and an alternative test appointment may be available to you.

Do not take the risk

Postpone your driving test rather than putting lives at risk.

Your instructor may offer you a 'mock test' shortly before your real test is due. This will give you an understanding of how the test will be conducted and may alert you to a weakness.

Make sure you understand what you are asked to do and, should you need to work on any difficulties you experience, work with your instructor on training to overcome them.

The Test Appointment

When your application has been received, you will be sent notification.

It will give the date, time and place of your appointment.

This also acts as a receipt for your fee.

Check your appointment notification as soon as you receive it to make sure the date and time of the test appointment are suitable.

If you do not receive notification after 21 days, contact the DSA Regional Office as soon as possible.

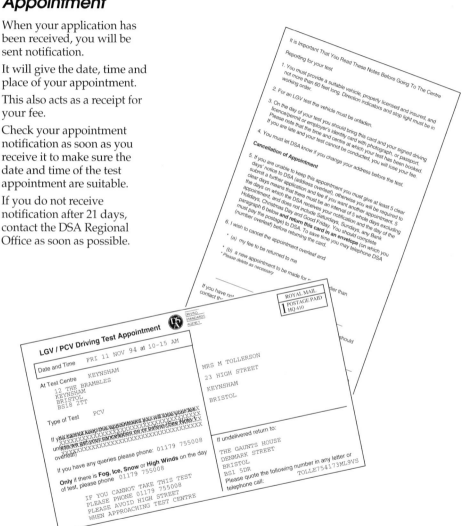

2

Cancellations

If you cannot keep the appointment, you should notify the DSA Regional Office immediately and return your appointment notification.

You must give at least **5** clear (working) days' notice, otherwise you will forfeit your fee and will have to re-apply with another fee.

Note: 5 clear days means an interval of 5 whole working days

- not counting the day DSA Regional Office receives your notification

- not counting the day of your test.

Change of Address

Please notify the DSA Regional Office immediately if you change your address before the day of your appointment

Change of Vehicle

Please notify the DSA Regional Office if you have to bring a different vehicle from the one described on your application form in order to avoid delay when you arrive for your test.

Inform the driving examiner at the test centre, either beforehand, or as soon as you arrive, if there is any last-minute change of vehicle.

To drive a bus, coach and some midi-and mini-buses unaccompanied, you must first pass the driving test.

This section sets out the main requirements of the test.

The way the special exercises are carried out depends on whether it is conducted by a DSA examiner or a delegated company one, as explained in Chapter 8. In all other respects the tests are the same.

Do not think of it as just a longer version of the car driving test which the learner driver faces – you will be expected to drive in a thoroughly expert and professional manner.

The PCV Driving Test

2

The test lasts about one and a half hours and legally must include :

Special exercises

- a reversing exercise
- a braking exercise
- a gearchanging exercise.

On the Road

- a drive including a wide variety of road and traffic conditions – of approximately one hour duration.

The route will take in roads carrying two-way traffic, dual carriageways, and where possible, one-way systems.

You will be expected to demonstrate that you can move off smoothly and safely both uphill and downhill, in addition to moving off normally ahead and at an angle

You will also need to show that you can safely

- meet other vehicles
- overtake
- cross the path of other vehicles
- keep a safe separation distance
- negotiate various types of roundabouts
- exercise correct lane discipline
- display courtesy and consideration to other road users especially:
  - pedestrians
  - riders on horseback
  - cyclists
  - motorcyclists
- apply the correct procedure at
  - pedestrian crossings
  - level crossings (both railway and tramway – where appropriate)
  - traffic signals
  - road junctions.

You will need to show

- effective use of the mirrors
- correct use of signals
- alertness and anticipation
- correct use of speed
- observance of speed limits
- vehicle sympathy.

Questions will be asked based on

- *The Highway Code*
- Other matters relating to safe operation and driving.

Attending for the test

PCV driving tests are conducted to a strict timetable.

Make sure you arrive in good time – otherwise your test cannot be taken and you will lose your fee.

The test will last for 1½ hrs – make sure that you will not exceed the number of hours you are allowed to drive by law and that you have sufficient fuel.

Upon meeting the PCV examiner, you will be asked to sign a declaration that the vehicle you are using for your test is fully insured for that purpose.

You must also satisfy the examiner of your identity.

Your Licences

Make sure you have

- your full motor car licence (Category B)
- the appropriate PCV licence entitlement

  – provisional

or

  – full PCV (or PSV) for a category which gives you provisional entitlement.

It is your responsibility to ensure that you have the appropriate licence entitlement.

If you have any reason to believe you may not be granted a licence to drive PCVs

or

your licence has been returned to DVLA Swansea for any reason, you must inform the examiner **before** the start of the test.

If you don't have your driving licence(s) with you, the examiner will ask you for some other form of identity.

Any of the following are acceptable:

- a signed driving licence issued in any other country provided it bears

  – your name in the roman alphabet

  and

  – your photograph

or

- your signed passport

or

- your signed International Driving Permit

or

- your signed British Forces driving licence

or

- a signed identity card issued to you by your employer. This must show

  – your name in the roman alphabet and

  – your photograph.

The examiner might not be able to conduct your test if you are unable to produce one of these documents.

Preparing your Vehicle

2

To avoid wasting your own time and the examiner's, make sure that the vehicle :

- has no passengers (see page 91)

- is in the category for which you wish to hold a licence

- does not exceed 60 feet in length (18.28m)

- has L-plates visible to the front and to the rear

- is not being used on a Trade Licence or displaying trade registration plates

- has a secure seat for the examiner from which he or she can observe the driver.

It would be unusual for you or your vehicle not to meet the above requirements, but where vehicles have been adapted for other purposes they may not be suitable for the purposes of the test for these or other reasons. If you are in doubt, ask DSA.

Make sure your vehicle has enough fuel not only for the test (at least 20 miles) but also for you to return to base.

You will be asked to carry out a gear-changing exercise during the test unless your vehicle is fitted with automatic transmission.

Some modern vehicles with automated and semi-automatic gear shifting systems **may not** be suitable for a manual test unless the driver is able to select the gears requested by the examiner and is required to use a clutch pedal whilst moving off, stopping and changing gear.

Safety Checks

Make sure that your vehicle is in a thoroughly roadworthy condition especially:

- stop lamps
- direction indicators
- lenses/reflectors
- mirrors
- brakes
- tyres
- exhaust/silencer
- windscreen/washer /wipers.

Preliminaries

The examiner will not conduct an eyesight test at the start of your test because you have already met the eyesight and medical requirements before your PCV provisional entitlement was granted.

Before you start the engine

The examiner expects that you have checked and prepared your bus for driving and for taking your test. You are not expected to do a time consuming or extensive check when he or she is with you.

However, before you start your engine you must always be sure that:

- all doors are properly closed
- your seat is correctly adjusted and comfortable so that
  - you can reach all controls easily
  - you have good all round vision
- your driving mirrors are correctly adjusted
- if fitted, your seat belt is fastened, correctly adjusted, and comfortable
- the handbrake is on
- the gear lever is in neutral.

So develop good habits and practise them while you are learning.

The examiner will not be impressed if you have to make adjustments during the test which should have been carried out before it began.

After you start the engine

Do not attempt to drive a vehicle fitted with air brakes until the gauges show the correct pressure, or if any warning device (a buzzer sounding or a light flashing) is operating.

If you are driving a vehicle with automatic transmission you should make sure that the safety checks which apply to your vehicle have been carried out.

2

The Reversing Exercise

2

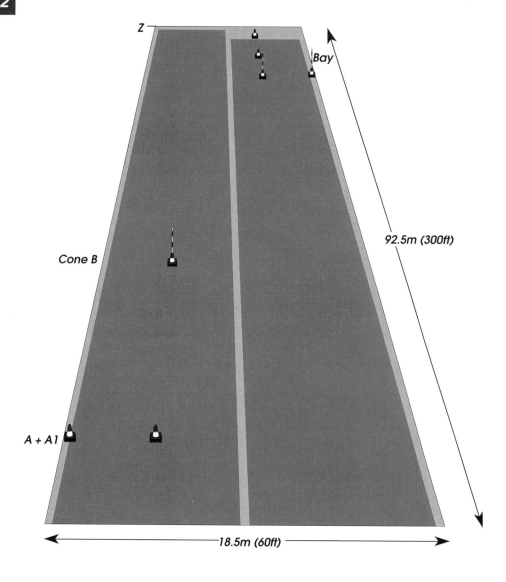

Z

Bay

92.5m (300ft)

Cone B

A + A1

18.5m (60ft)

The Reversing Exercise

If you take the test with a delegated company examiner the reversing exercise may consist of reversing into side roads on the left and right during the 'on road' part of the test. The examiner will explain in detail what is expected and your trainer will help you to prepare.

Otherwise you will do an 'off road' reversing exercise at the start of the test.

The diagram opposite shows the area layout for this exercise.

The exercise is to test your ability to manoeuvre your vehicle in areas where there is not much room. You must avoid marker posts and back into a clearly defined bay:

- under control
- with reasonable accuracy
- with effective observation throughout
- starting from a fixed point (Cones A and A1).

keeping *inside* a clearly defined boundary

- so that the offside of your vehicle clears Cone B
- stopping with the extreme rear of your vehicle within the solid (yellow painted) box area

at the end of the bay formed by cones.

The examiner will use a diagram of the manoeuvring area to explain the exercise to you.

The manoeuvring area is 92.5 metres long by 18.5 metres wide (300ft by 60ft)

There is a yellow boundary line.

Note: At some centres, there is a steel barrier along part of the boundary.

Vehicles without a significant front overhang

Cone 'A' is positioned on the area boundary.

Vehicles with a front overhang

The examiner has the discretion to move cones 'A' and 'A1' and cone 'B' 1 metre further into the area from the boundary line, if the front axle is well back from the front of the bus or if it has a limited turning circle.

Distances

A - A1 = 1½ times width of vehicle

A - B = twice the length of vehicle

B - line Z = 3 times length of vehicle

(overall length for the manoeuvre will be 5 times length of the vehicle)

The width of bay will be 1½ times the width of the vehicle.

The length of bay will be based on the length of the vehicle.

This can be varied at the discretion of the examiner so that the bay is one of the following lengths

- 1 metre (3 feet approx) longer than your vehicle
- the same length as your vehicle
- 1 metre shorter than your vehicle
- 2 metres (6 feet approx) shorter than your vehicle.

You will not be told the precise length of the bay, as part of this exercise is designed to assess your judgement of the size of your vehicle.

2

Skills you must acquire

The examiner will ask you to drive your bus from the place you have parked it up to cones A and A1 when he or she signals you to do so.

Drive up to the cones and stop so that

- the front of your bus is between but not beyond the cones

- the bus is more or less parallel with the yellow edge line.

If you do not do this the examiner may have to ask you to re-position your vehicle.

When you are asked, you should then

- apply the appropriate amount of steering lock so that the offside of your bus passes clear of cone 'B' (which also has a marker pole)

- drive across the area at a reasonable pace in reverse gear until the rear of your bus enters the bay formed by cones (the two cones at the entrance to the bay will have marker poles).

- carefully control your use of the accelerator, clutch and foot-brake throughout

- steer to position your vehicle accurately

- make effective observations throughout the exercise

- make smooth continuous progress across the area

- stop in the positions explained to you by the examiner.

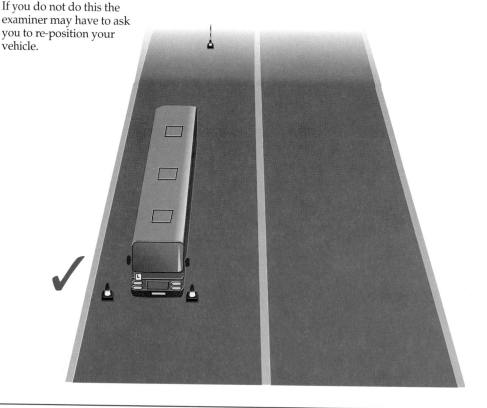

Faults you should avoid

- approaching the starting point too fast
- not driving in a reasonably straight line as you approach
- stopping beyond the first marker cones 'A' and 'A1'
- turning the steering wheel the wrong way, or turning too much or not enough when starting to reverse
- oversteering so that the front offside wheel travels outside the yellow boundary line of the area (at some PCV test centres, there are steel barriers along the perimeter of the area!)
- not taking effective observation or misjudging the position of your vehicle so that it hits (or is about to drive over) Cone 'B' + marker pole

- not taking effective observation or misjudging the position of your vehicle so that it hits (or is about to drive over) the cones or marker poles making up the bay
- allowing the wheel(s) of your vehicle to ride over the boundary lines of the bay or the area
- incorrect judgement so that the rear of your vehicle is either short of, or beyond, the yellow box area at the end of the bay (again, most PCV test centres have steel barriers at the end of this bay!)

- taking **excessive** steering movements or 'shunts' to complete the manoeuvre – since an overall high standard is expected, only a minimal number of shunts will be accepted
- driving down the area ahead of a position level with cones 'A' and 'A1' when you are 'shunting.'

This is because you will have gone outside the limits set for your vehicle (i.e its length × 5) after starting the exercise

- carrying out the manoeuvre at an excessively slow pace
- leaving the cab in order to satisfy yourself of the vehicle's position.

You should remember, that, throughout the test, the examiner will be looking for expert handling of the controls.

The Braking Exercise

2

This exercise usually takes place on the special manoeuvring area at the test centre and not on the public roads.

The examiner will be with you in the vehicle for the braking exercise.

You should make sure before you come to the test, that there is no loose equipment in the interior of the bus, or in luggage lockers etc. which may fly about and cause injury or damage during this exercise.

Two marker cones approximately 61m (200 feet) away will pointed out to you.

You should build up the speed of the vehicle to about 32 kph (20 mph).

Only when the front of your vehicle passes between the two markers should you apply the brakes.

You should stop quickly, safely and with the bus under full control.

If your test is conducted by a delegated examiner, the braking exercise may be carried out on a quiet public road, and the examiner will make sure that no other traffic is close enough to be inconvenienced.

The signal to stop will be explained to you. Make sure that you understand what it will be.

The signal used depends on the type of vehicle, so it may be the examiner saying 'stop!' loudly or it may be a bell signal.

Skills you must acquire

Stopping the vehicle

- as quickly as possible
- under full control
- as safely as possible
- in a straight line.

Faults you should avoid

- driving too slowly (less than 32 kph (20 mph))
- braking too soon (anticipating the marker points or the signal)
- braking too harshly causing skidding
- being too late depressing the clutch and possibly stalling the engine
- being too early depressing the clutch and failing to take full advantage of any engine braking.

If your bus is fitted with any additional braking controls such as a retarder, exhaust brake, or emergency air brake you are not expected to use them in this exercise, as it is a test of your ability to stop quickly under normal circumstances.

2

The Vehicle Controls

What the test requires

You must show the examiner that you understand what all the controls do and that you can use them

- smoothly
- correctly
- skilfully
- safely
- at the right time.

In particular, the examiner must be sure that you can properly control the

- accelerator
- clutch
- footbrake
- handbrake
- steering
- gears.

If your vehicle has automatic transmission, some of these will not, of course, apply to you.

You must

- understand what these controls do
- be able to use them competently.

How the examiner will test you

For this aspect of driving there is no special exercise (except for the gear exercise).

The examiner will watch you carefully to see how you use these controls.

Accelerator, clutch, gears and brakes

Skills you must aquire

- balancing the accelerator and clutch to pull away smoothly
- accelerating evenly to gain speed
- releasing the accelerator carefully to avoid jerky driving
- when stopping the bus, press the clutch in just before the vehicle stops
- engaging the clutch smoothly and carefully.

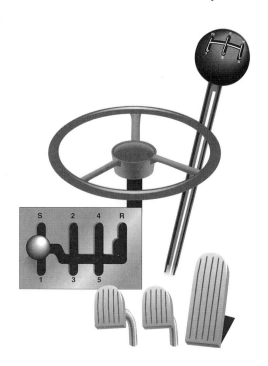

Faults you should avoid

- loud over-revving, so that you alarm or distract other road users – causing excessive engine noise and resulting exhaust fumes
- heavy, inappropriate acceleration, followed by immediate braking
- making the bus jerk and lurch through uncontrolled use of the accelerator or the clutch.
- 'riding' the clutch – that is failing to take your foot off the pedal when not using it.
- jerky and uncontrolled use of the clutch when moving off or changing gear.

Manual Gearboxes

2 The gears are designed to assist the engine to deliver power under a variety of conditions.

The lowest gears may only be necessary if the vehicle is loaded, or when climbing steep gradients. You should be aware of the manufacturer's advice for the particular vehicle you are driving. Some suggest that first gear should always be used when pulling away, whilst others advise second.

Following this advice can save your company a lot of money in minimising gearbox wear.

Skills you must aquire

- moving off in the most suitable gear
- choosing the most appropriate gear for your speed and the road conditions
- changing gear in good time before a hazard or junction
- on gradients, it is essential to plan well ahead – whether climbing, or before starting to descend a long hill.

If you leave it until you are either losing or gaining too much speed, you may have difficulty selecting gear and maintaining control

Faults you should avoid

- taking your eyes off the road when you change gear
- coasting with
  - the clutch pedal depressed

or
  - the gear lever in neutral.

This is particularly dangerous in vehicles fitted with air brakes since the engine-driven compressor will not replace air being exhausted as the brakes are applied, due to the engine only running at 'tickover' speed.

- holding on to the gear lever unnecessarily
- selecting the 'wrong' gear.

Automatic gearboxes

Modern vehicles may be fitted with sophisticated systems controlled by on-board computers.

These systems sense the load, speed, gradient etc. and select the most appropriate gear for the conditions.

FORWARD

NEUTRAL

REVERSE

SECOND

LOW

On such systems, the driver may only have to ease the accelerator, or depress the clutch pedal to allow the system to engage the gear required.

Some automatic gearboxes are controlled by a very simple three button system

- forward (drive)
- neutral
- reverse.

Even so, it is essential that you learn the correct way to use the system

Some systems have a 'kick-down' facility whereby a lower gear can be engaged to allow rapid acceleration (for overtaking, for instance). This is achieved by pressing the accelerator to the floor.

Skills you must acquire

- holding the vehicle firmly on the footbrake before pressing 'forward' to engage the drive
  - Some systems have interlocks which prevent drive being engaged unless the brake pedal is depressed or the doors closed etc.
- pressing the selector buttons only when the bus is completely stationary
- making careful use of the accelerator to ensure smooth automatic gearchanging.

Faults you should avoid

- engaging drive whilst the engine 'revs' are above tickover
- letting the bus remain stationary for long periods with 'forward' or 'reverse'engaged
- forgetting to engage 'drive' before attempting to move off
- not making proper use of any 'kick-down' facility.

2

Semi-automatic gearboxes

The system most commonly found on buses and coaches is one whereby the driver has full control over the gear selected but has no clutch pedal.

This is often a 'pneumo-cyclic' gearbox which consists of a number of electronic relays controlling air systems which do the actual gear changes.

When coupled with a fluid fly-wheel this eliminates the need for a clutch when pulling away, stopping or changing gear.

The gears are chosen by means of a 'gate' selector, and smooth changes require some skill and practice to achieve.

Again, the most appropriate method of changing gear will depend on the manufacturer's advice for the particular vehicle. Most advise that a brief pause be made when the lever is in neutral when changing between one gear and another. The accelerator should be set at a level appropriate for the gear about to be engaged.

Usually semi-automatic gearboxes are coupled to diesel engines and the amount of time needed in neutral to allow the engine revs to match the road speed needs careful consideration.

Skills you must acquire

• holding the vehicle firmly on the footbrake before engaging forward or reverse gears from standstill

– Some systems have interlocks which prevent drive being engaged unless the brake pedal is depressed or the doors closed etc.

• making careful use of the accelerator to ensure smooth gearchanging.

Faults you should avoid

• engaging a forward or reverse gear from standsill whilst the engine 'revs' are above tickover

• letting the bus remain stationary for long periods with a forward gear or 'reverse' engaged

• forgetting to engage a gear before attempting to move off

• not making proper use of the gear selector and accelerator.

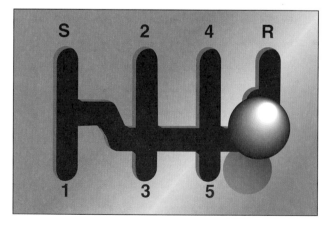

Footbrake

Because most buses, coaches and midibuses are equipped with airbrake systems, there is frequently no direct relationship between the pressure applied to the pedal and the braking force exerted on the wheels.

This means that good control is needed at all times when braking.

Vehicles equipped with disc brakes permit a technique in which the pressure applied to the brake pedal is proportional to the braking effect applied to the wheels, as does the hydraulic system fitted to some minibuses.

Older vehicles may have vacuum brake systems which have similar characteristics to air brakes.

Some vehicles may have a system known as 'air-over-hydraulic' in which air pressure operates a hydraulic braking system. These are usually lighter vehicles and the system is designed to make the brakes less harsh.

Skills you must acquire

• braking in good time
• braking lightly in most situations
• braking progressively
• the correct technique for releasing pressure on the brake just before coming to rest. This allows you to stop the bus without jerks.

Faults you should avoid

• braking harshly
• excessive and prolonged use of the footbrake
• braking and steering at the same time unless already travelling at low speed
• braking in a way which would cause passengers discomfort.

2

Handbrake

Buses, coaches and minibuses are equipped with one of two types of handbrake.

* Mechanical
  - generally found on older or smaller vehicles
  - have a long lever with a button or, more usually, a squeeze grip release, as in a car. The lever pulls a series of cables which apply the rear (or, more rarely, the front) brakes

* Air operated
  - fitted to vehicles with air, or air-over-hydraulic footbrake systems
  - operated by a small lever with a collar or push button release

Skills you must acquire

* knowing how and when to apply the handbrake.

Some modern braking systems will apply a parking brake when the vehicle is brought to a stop by the footbrake. The handbrake is released in the normal way. You should know how to operate this system if it is fitted to a vehicle you intend to drive

* applying the handbrake when you intend to secure the vehicle before leaving the cab.

* co-ordinating your use of the handbrake and other controls in order to achieve smooth uphill starts.

Faults you should avoid

* never apply the handbrake before the vehicle has stopped

* never try to move off with the handbrake on

* on automatic vehicles with a 'Park' position on the gear selector the gearbox locks when 'P' is engaged. This must not be used as a substitute for applying the handbrake, as the vehicle may be free to move when the next driver selects neutral to start the engine!

* in manual buses and coaches excessive clutch wear will result from 'holding' the vehicle on the clutch on uphill slopes. The clutch is not designed to transmit the force required to stop up to 18 tons from moving backwards! You should always apply the handbrake and carry out the correct uphill start procedure to avoid this.

Emergency Brakes

All vehicles have to have at least two braking systems so that failure of one will not prevent the vehicle being brought to rest safely.

Modern vehicles have sophisticated braking systems which may include anti-lock and automatic load compensating valves.

'Split' systems are often fitted to ensure that failure of one part of the normal braking system can leave other parts operational.

'Fail safe' systems can result in the automatic gradual application of all or some of the brakes if the driver ignores brake warning indicators.

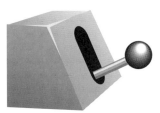

Construction and Use regulations require the driver to be able to apply all or part of the braking system in the event of footbrake failure.

In simple terms this means that, if you press the footbrake and nothing happens, you must have another way of stopping.

How you can do this depends on the system fitted.

- Mechanical handbrakes – the handbrake can be applied progressively to bring the bus to a stop.

- Emergency brake – a separate lever is provided on some older air and vacuum braked buses to allow progressive application of the brakes.

- Air operated handbrake – the brake is partially applied to allow progressive application of the brakes.

During your training you should find out which method should be used with the vehicle you are driving and you should practise it in a safe place, preferably off the road and under expert supervision.

2

You must not use this method of braking at any time during your test. The braking exercise in the driving test requires a rapid, controlled stop, using the footbrake. It is NOT an emergency stop exercise.

Skills you must acquire

- you must use skill and vehicle sympathy to gauge the degree of application required to achieve a safe stop.

Faults you should avoid

- immediate full application of the brake
- locking the wheels and skidding
- coming to rest heavily in a way which may injure passengers.

2

Steering

The bus, coach or minibus you drive will probably have power assisted steering – but it may not.

With power assistance the steering effort required is greatly reduced through the action of an engine driven pump.

It is generally necessary to take corners more slowly when you do not have the benefit of power assistance, simply because the gearing at the steering wheel is lower and it takes more effort and more time to turn it.

The danger with power assistance is that the lack of effort required (and in some cases, the lack of 'feel' transmitted back to the driver) can result in taking corners too quickly for either safety or comfort. You need to be aware of this.

Skills you must acquire

• placing your hands on the steering wheel in a position which is comfortable and which gives you full control at all times

• keeping your steering movements steady and smooth

• being aware of the 'swept path' your vehicle will take and steer an accurate path.

It is particularly important to take the correct path when driving a bus with long overhangs or limited ground clearance

Faults you must avoid

• turning the wheel too early when taking a corner.

If you do, you risk

– cutting the corner when turning right causing the rear wheel(s) to cut across the path of traffic waiting to emerge

– striking the kerb when turning left

• turning too late

You could put other road users at risk by

– swinging wide at left turns

– overshooting right turns

• crossing your hands on the steering wheel (whenever possible)

• allowing the wheel to spin back after turning

• resting your arm on the door

Remember:

The stability of a bus can be affected by cornering too quickly.

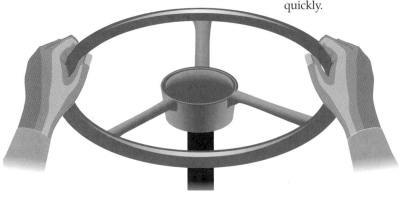

The other controls

You must understand

- the functions of all controls and switches which have a bearing on road safety, for example
  - indicators
  - lights
  - windscreen wipers
  - demisters
- the meaning of gauges or other displays on the instrument panel, especially
  - air pressure gauge(s)
  - speedometer
  - various warning lights/buzzers
  - on-board computer displays
  - brake systems failure warnings
  - bulb failure warnings
  - gear selection indicators
- time, speed and distance recording equipment, including
  - operating tachographs
  - completing tachograph charts
  - keeping records
  - the operation of any speed limiting equipment fitted.

Safety checks

You should also be able to

- carry out routine safety checks
  - oil and coolant levels
  - tyre pressures
- identify defects, especially with
  - steering
  - brakes
  - tyres
  - seat belts
  - lights
  - reflectors
  - horn
  - rear view mirrors
  - speedometer
  - exhaust system
  - direction indicators
  - windscreen, wipers and washers
  - wheel nut security
- understand the effects which any fault or defect will have on the handling of your vehicle.

Warning

Note that some bus manufacturers, but not all, fit wheel nuts which tighten clockwise on the nearside of the vehicle and anti-clockwise on the offside. Make sure that you know which thread is fitted to your vehicle before you attempt to tighten them. The consequences of getting it wrong are unthinkable. In any case, it is much better to entrust this to trained mechanics wherever possible, as the nuts should always be tightened to the specified torque.

Some wheels are 'spigot' mounted and require specialised knowledge when being removed or re-fitted.

2

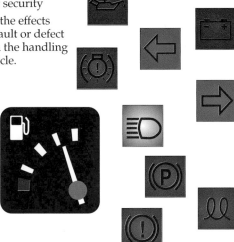

Moving off from standstill

What the test requires

You must be able to move off safely and under control

- on the level
- from behind a parked vehicle
- on a hill
- uphill and downhill.

How the examiner will test you

The examiner will watch your use of the controls each time you move off.

Level and uphill starts

- Aim to co-ordinate your use of the controls so that the bus remains stationary momentarily when the handbrake is released, ready to move off.
- You should complete your checks and ensure that the road ahead is clear.
- If there is more than a moment's delay between releasing the brake and moving off, re-apply the handbrake and repeat the sequence when it is safe to do so.

Downhill starts

- Prevent the bus from moving when you release the handbrake by applying the footbrake first.

Angle starts

- Ensure that you apply sufficient steering to pass the parked vehicle safely.
- Ensure that you will not endanger approaching traffic when you move.

Skills you must acquire

- watching the road ahead and behind in order to predict an opportunity to move.
- when you see that you will shortly be able to move off
  - selecting an appropriate gear or 'drive' and preparing the vehicle to move
  - checking whether it is safe to move off, and informing other road users of your intentions by
  - using your mirrors
  - signalling if necessary
  - releasing the handbrake, then just before you move off, looking round for
    - other vehicles
    - cyclists
    - pedestrians or animals outside the range of your mirrors
  - checking the road immediately ahead and moving off under control making balanced and safe use of
    - the accelerator
    - the clutch
    - the brakes
    - the steering.

Faults you should avoid

- forgetting to engage a forward gear
- moving off whilst looking back
- failing to co-ordinate your use of the controls to achieve a safe, comfortable start
- endangering other road users when moving off
- not coordinating the accelerator, clutch and handbrake with the result that the vehicle
  - stalls
  - rolls backwards on an uphill slope
  - surges away.

As you move off and the position of the vehicle on the road changes, re-check all your mirrors to ensure that all is well, both outside and inside the vehicle, but do not allow this to distract you when your attention should be on the road ahead.

The Gear Changing Exercise

2

The examiner will ask you to pull up at a convenient place to carry out the gear changing exercise (usually at an early stage in the test).

You will be asked to move off in the lowest gear and change up to each gear in turn until you reach a gear the examiner considers appropriate for your vehicle.

This will depend on the gearbox fitted and the examiner will make sure that you understand which gear should be reached.

When you are in that gear, the examiner will want to see you change back down into each gear in turn, driving for a short distance in each one until you reach the lowest gear again.

You will not be asked to select either

- a particular ratio if the vehicle is fitted with a two-speed axle

or

- a particular range if the gearbox has low and high range selection.

The gear changing exercise is to allow the examiner to see you engage the lower gears (which you may not otherwise need to use during the test) competently.

You will not be asked to use anything other than the normal gears appropriate to your vehicle.

Skills you must acquire

- moving off smoothly in the lowest gear
- changing up to the next gear as soon as the correct speed is reached
- smooth, unhurried and precise gearchanges
- when changing down, matching the road speed of the vehicle to the lower gear by careful use of the footbrake, if necessary.

Throughout this exercise, you must

- take effective observation, especially before moving off and slowing down
- give any signal which may be appropriate
- use the controls skilfully to ensure smooth engagement of the gears.

Faults you should avoid

- not showing sufficient consideration for other road users before moving off, during the exercise or when slowing down by
  - forgetting to check the mirrors
  - not acting sensibly in response to the actions of other drivers
  - not signalling to inform other road users before moving off or slowing down
- jerky use of the accelerator or clutch
- not starting off in the lowest gear
- not selecting the next gear in sequence
- not being able to engage a gear
- not slowing the bus down enough before selecting a low gear.

2

Using the mirrors

Mirrors are one of the best aids to road safety fitted to any vehicle. They help you to avoid causing problems to other road users and allow you to predict when to take action safely.

Try not to think of mirror checks as something you do because you have been told to. The important point is not that you have looked in the mirrors, but that you have gained additional information to help you to drive safely.

Try to time your mirror checks to allow time to assess what you see **BEFORE** taking any action.

What the test requires

Make sure you use your mirrors effectively

- before any manoeuvre
- to keep up to date on what is happening behind you

Check carefully before

- moving off
- signalling
- changing direction
- turning left or right
- overtaking or changing lanes
- increasing speed
- slowing down or stopping
- opening any offside door.

Check again in the nearside mirror after

- passing parked vehicles
- passing horse riders, motorcyclists, or cyclists
- passing any pedestrians standing close to the kerb
- passing any vehicle you have just overtaken – **before** moving back to the left.

How the examiner will test you

For this aspect of driving, there is no special exercise.

The examiner will watch your use of mirrors as you drive.

Skills you must acquire

- establishing good habits by
  - looking before you signal
  - looking and signalling before you act
  - acting sensibly and safely on what you see in the mirrors
- being aware that the mirrors will not show everything behind you

- checking your nearside mirror every time after passing
  - parked vehicles
  - vulnerable road users
  - vehicles you have just overtaken
- always being as aware of what is happening behind you and alongside, as you are of what is going on ahead.
- always being aware of the effect your bus has on any vulnerable road users you may pass.

Faults you should avoid

- manoeuvring without checking the mirrors first
- not acting on what you see when you look in the mirrors
- taking action at the same time as looking in the mirrors instead of as a result of what you see in them
- looking in the mirrors at an inappropriate moment, so that you don't notice something important ahead.

Remember that just looking is not enough!

It is what you see that is important.

Always use the

Mirrors
Signal
Manoeuvre (MSM)

Position
Speed
Look (PSL)

routine.

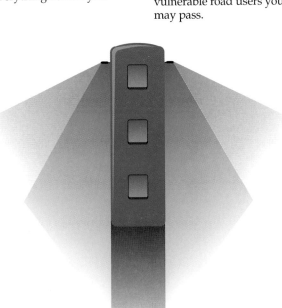

Sequence of mirror checks

Professional drivers develop a technique for checking mirrors whilst remaining fully aware of what is happening ahead.

Whatever method you adopt the examiner will only be concerned that you are making proper use of the mirrors and acting sensibly on what you see in them, whilst remaining aware of what is happening ahead at all times.

When you are on the road, hazards and the need to begin a manoeuvre to deal with them often occur together, or one immediately after another.

You must be sure that your technique ensures that you observe every potential danger and are fully prepared to deal with them if they occur.

The sequence of checks is complicated to describe, and has to be adapted as situations develop. In reality it takes only moments to do and should become second nature without the need to constantly analyse what you are doing.

Order of checks

- identify the hazard which gives rise to the need to manoeuvre

- assess where the greater potential danger lies in the manouevre about to be carried out, to the right or to the left of the bus and check that mirror

- check the mirror on the other side

- as your eyes return to looking ahead, re-assess the hazard and, if you have a central mirror which allows you to see what is happening behind, check the position of following traffic

- check the other mirror and, as your eyes return to looking ahead, assess what you have seen and signal if necesary

- carry out the manoeuvre, rechecking the mirrors as necessary.

Example – moving out to pass a parked car

See the parked car some distance ahead

2

The primary danger is that someone may attempt to overtake you as you need to move out. Check the offside mirror

Check the nearside mirror

Check that the parked car has not moved away, or that you will need to give it extra room because someone is about to get out

Will you need to wait for approaching traffic?

See what traffic is following you by checking the offside mirror

Has the situation ahead changed?

Signal right, if necessary

Begin to move out, if it is safe to do so, or wait if it is not

Keep checking how the situation develops.

Giving signals

2

What the test requires

You must give clear signals in good time so that other road users know what you intend to do next.

This is particularly important with long PCVs because other road users may not understand the position you need to move into

- before turning left
- before turning right
- at roundabouts
- to move off at an angle
- before reversing into an opening.

You must only use the signals shown in *The Highway Code* as any others may be misunderstood.

Any signal you give must help other road users to

- understand what you intend to do next
- take appropriate action.

Always check that you have cancelled an indicator signal as soon as it is safe to do so.

How the examiner will test you

For this aspect of driving, there is no special exercise.

The examiner will watch carefully to see how you use signals in your driving.

Skills you must acquire

Giving any signals

- clearly
- at the appropriate time
- by indicator
- by arm, if necessary.

Make sure that any signal you give is displayed for long enough for other road users to see and understand its meaning.

Faults you should avoid

- Giving misleading signals
- Giving incorrect signals
- Omitting to cancel signals
- 'Waving on' pedestrians to cross in front of your vehicle (you or they may not have seen another danger which you are 'inviting' them towards)
- Giving signals other than those shown in *The Highway Code*.

Acting on traffic signs and signals

What the test requires

You must have a thorough knowledge of traffic signs, signals, and road markings, and be able to

- recognise them in good time

- take appropriate action on them.

At the start of the road section of the PCV driving test the examiner will ask you to continue to drive ahead, unless traffic signs indicate otherwise – or unless you are asked to turn left or right.

You will be given any direction to turn in good time – if you are not sure, ask the examiner to repeat the direction.

2

Traffic Lights

You must

- comply with traffic lights

- approach at such a speed that you can stop, if necessary, under full control

- only move forward at a green traffic light if

  - it is clear for you to do so

  - by doing so, your vehicle will not block the junction.

Signals by Authorised persons

You must comply with signals given by

- police officers

- traffic wardens

- school crossing patrols

- any authorised person controlling traffic e.g. at road repairs.

Signals given by other road users

You must watch for signals given by other road users and

- react safely

- take appropriate action

- anticipate their actions

- if necessary, give signals to any traffic following your vehicle which may not be able to see the signals given by a road user ahead of you.

This is particularly important when a vehicle or rider ahead is intending to turn right, and the size of your vehicle prevents traffic behind you from seeing their signal.

Making normal progress

The examiner will be looking for a high standard of driving from an experienced driver displaying safe, confident, defensive driving techniques.

You are not a 'learner driver' and you will not pass the test if you drive hesitantly or in a way which shows that you are not fully in control of your bus.

Because you are an experienced driver, and you are expected to drive accordingly, you must

- select a safe speed to suit road, weather and traffic conditions

- move away at junctions as soon as it is safe to do so

- avoid stopping unnecessarily

- make progress when conditions permit.

How the examiner will test you

For this aspect of driving there is no special exercise.

The examiner will watch your driving and will expect to see you

- making reasonable progress where conditions allow

- keeping up with the traffic flow when it is safe and legal to do so

- making positive, safe decisions when you can make progress.

Skills you must acquire

You must be able to

- drive at the appropriate speed depending on
  - the type of road
  - the traffic conditions
  - the weather conditions and visibility
- approach all hazards at a safe speed without
  - being unduly cautious
  - holding up following traffic unnecessarily.

Faults you should avoid

You must not

- drive so slowly that you hinder other traffic
- be overcautious or hesitant
- stop when you can see it is obviously clear and safe to go on.

2

2

Controlling your speed

What the test requires

You must make good progress along the road, taking into consideration

- the type of road
- the volume of traffic
- the weather conditions and the state of the road surface
- the braking characteristics of your vehicle
- speed limits which apply to your vehicle
- any hazards associated with the time of day (school times etc.).

How the examiner will test you

For this aspect of driving there is no special exercise.

The examiner will watch carefully your control of speed as you drive.

Skills you must acquire

You must at all times

- take great care in the use of speed
- drive at the appropriate speed to the traffic conditions
- be sure that you can stop safely in the distance you can see to be clear
- leave a safe separation distance between your vehicle and traffic ahead of you
- allow extra stopping distance on wet or slippery road surfaces
- observe speed limits which apply to your vehicle
- drive defensively and anticipate any hazards which could arise
- allow for other road users making mistakes.

Faults you should avoid

- driving too fast for the
  - road
  - traffic
  - weather
  conditions
- exceeding speed limits
- varying your speed erratically
- having to brake hard to avoid a situation ahead
- approaching bends, traffic signals, and any other hazards at too high a speed.

Keeping a safe separation distance

Always keep a safe separation distance between you and the vehicle in front.

What the test requires

You must always drive at such a speed that you can stop safely in the distance you can see to be clear.

In good weather conditions, leave a gap of at least one metre (or yard) for each MPH of your speed – or a two second time gap. In bad conditions leave at least double the distance, or a four second time gap.

In slow-moving congested traffic it may not be practical to leave as much space, but you must always be sure that you can stop safely whatever happens.

How the examiner will test you

For this aspect of driving there is no special exercise. The examiner will watch carefully and take account of your

- use of the MSM/PSL routine
- anticipation
- reaction to changing road and traffic conditions
- handling of the controls.

Skills you must acquire

You must

- be able to judge a safe separation distance between you and the vehicle ahead
- show correct use of the MSM routine - especially before reducing speed
- avoid the need to brake sharply if the vehicle in front slows down or stops
- take extra care when your view ahead is limited by large vehicles such as other buses or lorries.

Watch out for

- brake lights ahead
- direction indicators
- vehicles ahead braking without warning.

Faults you should avoid

- following too closely – 'tailgating' on roads carrying traffic at higher speeds
- braking suddenly
- swerving to avoid the vehicle in front slowing down or stopping
- being unable to leave side road junctions clear when a queue of traffic stops.

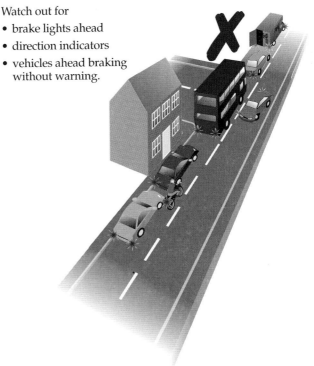

Hazards

2 *What is a hazard?*

When you are moving

A hazard is any situation which could involve adjusting speed or altering course.

Look well ahead where there are

- road junctions or roundabouts
- parked vehicles
- cyclists or horse riders
- pedestrian crossings.

By identifying the hazard early enough, you will have time to take the appropriate action.

When you are stationary

A hazard can be created by the actions of other road users around you.

Watch for

- pedestrians crossing in front
- cyclists or motorcyclists moving up alongside
- drivers edging up on the nearside before you make a left turn
- vehicles pulling up close behind when you intend to reverse.

Stay on the alert and watch what is happening around you!

Anticipation and Awareness

When driving in traffic the situation can change from second to second depending on the time of day, the location, and the density of traffic.

You can see that some things are obviously going to happen and the skilful driver anticipates what might happen !

As the driver of a bus, coach, or minibus you must constantly drive with this sense of awareness and anticipation by asking yourself

- what is happening ahead?
- what are other road users doing, or about to do?

- do I need to
  - speed up
  - slow down
  - prepare to stop
  - change direction?

It is essential to be fully alert at all times and constantly scan the road ahead. By doing this, you will remain in control of both the situation and your vehicle.

In fast-moving traffic you will need to be constantly checking and re-checking the scene around you. It is essential to recognise well in advance the mistakes other road users may be about to make.

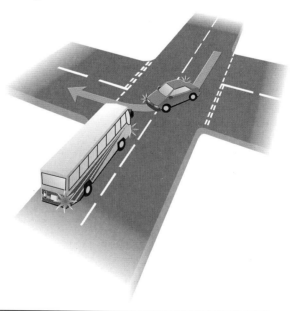

Hazards

Pedestrians

- Give way to pedestrians when turning from one road into another, or when entering premises such as supermarkets, shops warehouses etc.
- Take extra care with
  - the very young
  - the disabled
  - the elderly.

They may not realise you will not be able to stop suddenly!

You must be even more vigilant when driving through shopping areas where there are often large number of people waiting to cross at corners for example.

Drive slowly and considerately when you need to enter any pedestrianised areas.

Cyclists

Take extra care when

- crossing cycle lanes
- about to turn left and you can see a cyclist near the rear of your vehicle or moving up along the nearside.
- approaching any children on cycles
- there are gusty wind conditions.

Motorcyclists

Watch for motorcycles

- 'filtering' in slow traffic streams
- moving up along the side of your vehicle
- especially when you are about to move out at junctions.

Remember!

Think once

– Think twice

– Think bike!

Hazards

2

Riders and animals

Remember the size and noise and sometimes even the colour of your vehicle can unsettle even the best mannered horse – give riders as much room as you can.

Avoid the need to 'rev' the engine until you are clear. Several small applications of the brake as you approach will ensure that the air brake system relief valve does not 'blow off' just as you are level with the animal.

Watch young, possibly inexperienced riders, closely for signs of any difficulty with their mount.

React in good time to anyone herding animals.

Look out for warning signs or signals in rural districts.

Avoid

- Sounding the horn aggressively
- Revving the engine, deliberately
- Causing the air brakes to 'hiss', by heavy applications
- Edging forward when pedestrians are crossing in front of your vehicle
- Any signs of irritation or aggression towards other road users – especially the more vulnerable!

Correct road position and lane discipline

What the test requires

You should

- normally keep well to the left
- keep clear of parked vehicles
- avoid weaving in and out between parked vehicles
- position your vehicle correctly for the direction you intend to take
- obey road markings, especially
  - left and right turn arrows at junctions
  - when approaching roundabouts
  - in one-way streets
  - bus lanes
  - road markings for PCVs approaching arched or narrow low bridges.

With long PCVs, only straddle lane markings or move over to the left or right when necessary to avoid mounting the kerb or colliding with lamp-posts, traffic signs etc.

How the examiner will test you

For this aspect of driving there is no special exercise.

The examiner will watch carefully to see that you

- use the MSM routine
- select the correct lane in good time.

Skills you must acquire

You must

- use the MSM/PSL routine correctly
- plan ahead and choose the correct lane in good time
- position your vehicle sensibly – even if there are no lane markings shown
- always remember, other road users may not understand what you intend to do next. Watch them carefully and ensure that you signal in good time.

Faults you should avoid

- driving too close to the kerb
- driving too close to the centre of the road
- changing lanes at the last moment or without good reason
- hindering other road users by being badly positioned or in the wrong lane
- straddling lanes or lane markings when it is not necessary for you to do so
- using the size of your vehicle to block other road users from making progress
- cutting across the path of other road users in another lane at roundabouts.

2

Hazards

2 *Road Junctions*

Because of the size of your vehicle and the difficulties which may arise when manoeuvring a long bus, it is essential that at road junctions you get it right first time!

The main rule to apply is to never drive into a situation that you cannot see a clear path through.

If you have driven your bus into a blocked road, the traffic behind will prevent you from reversing out again and you are stuck.

Similarly, if you need to wait for an obstruction to clear stop in a position which allows you an 'escape route' if at all possible.

What the test requires

You should

- use the MSM/PSL routine in good time on approach

- assess the situation correctly, so that you can position the vehicle to negotiate the junction safely

- take as much room as you need on approach to see the road space available – there may be no room for a wide swing in the road you are entering

- take advantage of any improved vision from the driving position in your bus and stop or proceed as necessary

- be aware of any lane markings and the fact that your vehicle may have to occupy part of the lane alongside

- position as early as it is practicable to in one way streets

- make sure you take **effective** observation before emerging at any road junction

- use your mirrors to observe the rear wheels of your vehicle as you drive into and out of the junction

- assess the speed of oncoming vehicles correctly before crossing or entering roads with fast – moving traffic.

- always allow for the fact that you will need time to build up speed in the new road.

If you are crossing a dual carriageway, or turning right on to one, do not move forward unless you can clear the centre reservation safely. If your vehicle is too long for the gap, wait until it is clear from both sides and there is a safe opportunity to go.

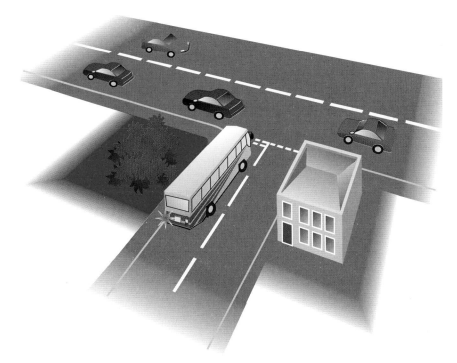

How the examiner will test you

For this aspect of driving there is no special exercise.

The examiner will watch carefully and take account of your

- use of the MSM/PSL routine
- position and speed on approach
- observation and judgement.

Remember!

Look well ahead on approach

Assess conditions at the junction

Decide when it is safe to go

Emerge safely at the junction or **E**nter the side road

Negotiate the hazard (junction) safely

This acronym recognises the difference in techniques between the PCV driver and the car driver and expands the

Look Assess Decide Act (LADA) procedure outlined in *The Driving Manual* [HMSO]

Hazards: Roundabouts

2

Roundabouts can vary in size and complexity but the object of all of them is to allow traffic to keep moving wherever possible.

Some roundabouts are so complex that they require traffic lights to control the volume of traffic, whilst at others 'part-time' signals operate only at peak periods.

At the majority of roundabouts the approaching traffic is required to give way to the traffic approaching from the right.

However, at some locations the 'Give Way' signs and markings apply to traffic already ON the roundabout and you must be aware of these differences.

It is essential that you plan your approach well in advance and use the MSM/PSL routine in good time.

With buses it is essential to adopt the appropriate lane depending on the exit you intend to take and the size of your vehicle.

Procedure

Unless lane markings or road signs indicate otherwise:

Turning Left

- check your mirrors
- give a left turn signal in good time as you approach
- approach in the left hand lane (with a long vehicle you may need to take some of the lane on your right – depending how sharp or narrow the exit turn is)
- adopt a path that ensures your rear wheels do not mount the kerb

- give way to traffic approaching from the right – if necessary
- use the nearside mirror(s) to be sure no cyclists/motorcyclists are trapped on the nearside
- use the offside mirror to check that no passing vehicle will be hit as the rear overhang swings out as you begin to turn
- continue to signal through the turn
- look well ahead for traffic islands/bollards in the middle of your exit road which will restrict the width available to you.

Going Ahead (Up to '12 o'clock')

You should

- approach in the left hand lane unless blocked or clearly marked for 'left turn' only

- do not give a signal on approach (other than brake lights if you need to reduce speed)

- try to stay in the lane – as far as is possible – depending on the length of your vehicle

- keep checking the mirrors – make sure that other road users anticipate the 'swept path' of your vehicle and be prepared to stop if they do not, as swerving will normally make matters worse

- indicate left as you pass the exit just before the one you intend to take

- look well ahead for traffic islands/bollards in the centre of your exit road

- make sure the rear wheels do not mount the kerb as you leave the roundabout.

Turning Right or Full circle (useful to turn PCVs)

You should

- look well ahead and use the MSM/PSL routine in good time

- signal right in good time before moving over to the right on approach and watch for any vehicles – especially motorcycles, accelerating up on the offside of your vehicle

- use the left hand of the two lanes with a long vehicle, if there is a choice of two lanes for turning right

- occupy part of the lane to your left if only one lane is marked for 'right turn' when you need extra space, not only on the approach, but also through the roundabout

- make frequent mirror checks

- only enter the roundabout when you are sure it is safe to emerge

- keep checking for traffic coming from your right.

On no account drive out across the path of any vehicle closely approaching from the right.

A bus, coach or tram emerging across an approaching driver's path will present a picture of up to 18 metres of steel chassis, side panels, passenger's faces at the windows and PCV sized wheels in front of their windscreen!

Not only could the approaching vehicle be travelling at speed, but it is also moving on a curved course and any sudden braking would be likely to send the vehicle into a skid.

- Use the mirrors to observe traffic coming round with you on the near side, and also that your rear wheels are keeping clear of the kerb on the roundabout itself

- Change the signal to left turn as you pass the exit before the one you wish to take.

Lane discipline on roundabouts

Plan well ahead.

Look out for traffic signs as you approach.

Have a clear picture of the exit you need to take.

Look for the number of exits before yours.

Either follow the lane markings as far as possible, or select the lane most suitable to the size of your vehicle.

Signal your intentions clearly and in good time.

Avoid driving into the roundabout too close to the right hand kerb.

It is not always possible to keep your vehicle within road markings. Make frequent mirror checks to ensure that you are not endangering others.

Assess the speed and intentions of traffic approaching from the right accurately.

Road surfaces

Roundabouts are junctions where considerable braking and acceleration takes place. The road surface can become slippery and polished, especially in wet weather.

Ensure all braking and speed reduction is done in good time.

If you can see it is clear to enter the roundabout, do so provided you will not cause any traffic from your right to brake or swerve.

2

Defensive driving

Always watch any vehicle in front when you are about to enter the roundabout.

Make sure it has moved off while you look to the right!

Drivers sometimes change their minds at the last moment.

Many rear-end collisions take place in just these circumstances.

Cyclists and horse riders

It is often safest for cyclists and horse riders to take the outside path when turning right at large roundabouts.

Watch for any signals and give them as much room as you safely can.

Multiple roundabouts

In a number of (usually well-known) locations, complex roundabout systems have been designed which incorporate a mini-roundabout at each exit.

The main thing to remember at such places is that traffic is travelling **in all directions.**

Mini roundabouts

The same rules apply at mini roundabouts.

Give way to traffic approaching from the right.

Because of the restricted space both entering and leaving these locations, it is essential to keep a constant check on the mirrors.

The rear of a long vehicle can easily 'clip' a car waiting to enter the mini-roundabout.

It is most unlikely that PCVs will be able to turn at a mini-roundabout without driving over the marked centre area.

Position your vehicle so that it does not drive over the kerb at the entrance or exit.

Double mini-roundabouts

These require even more care and planning since traffic will often back up from one to the other at busy times.

Make sure that there is room for you to move forward and that by doing so, your vehicle will not block the whole system.

Although traffic is advised not to carry out 'U' turn manoeuvres at a mini-roundabout, be alert for any oncoming traffic doing so.

Because of the limited space and the comparatively short amount of time it takes to negotiate a mini-roundabout,

it is important to give only signals which will help other road users.

Avoid any signals which might confuse.

If you have to drive over a raised mini-roundabout, do so slowly and carefully so as not to damage your bus or cause discomfort to passengers

At any roundabout, cancel your indicator signal as soon as you have completed the manoeuvre.

Hazards

2 | ### Overtaking other road users

What the test requires

When overtaking, you must

- look well ahead for any hazards such as
  - oncoming traffic
  - bends
  - junctions
  - road markings
  - traffic signs
  - the vehicle in front about to overtake
  - any gradient
- assess the speed of the vehicle you intend to overtake
- assess the speed differential of the two vehicles. This will indicate how long the manoeuvre could take
- allow enough room to overtake safely
- avoid the need to 'cut in' on the vehicle you have just overtaken.

How the examiner will test you

For this aspect of driving there is no special exercise.

The examiner will watch carefully and take account of your

- use of the MSM/PSL routine
- reactions to road and traffic conditions
- handling of the controls
- choice of safe opportunities to overtake.

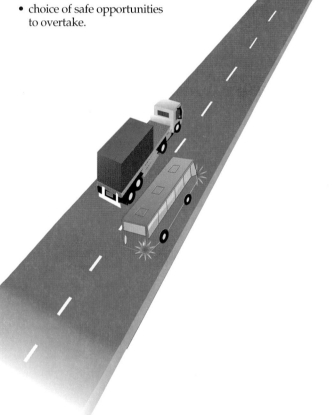

Skills you must acquire

You must be able to assess ALL the factors which will decide if you can or cannot overtake safely such as

- oncoming traffic
- the type of road (single or dual carriageway)
- the speed of the vehicle ahead
- if you can overtake before reaching any continuous white line on your side of the road
- how far ahead the road is clear
- whether the road will remain clear
- your mirror check shows that there is traffic behind about overtake your own vehicle.

Overtake only when you can do so

- safely
- legally
- without causing other road users to slow down or alter course.

Faults you should avoid

You must not overtake when

- your view of the road ahead is not clear
- you would have to exceed the speed limit
- to do so would cause other road users to slow down, stop, or swerve
- there are signs or road markings which prohibit overtaking.

2

Hazards

2

Meeting other vehicles and passing stationary vehicles

What the test requires

You must be able to meet and deal with oncoming traffic safely and confidently, especially

- on narrow roads
- where there are obstructions such as parked cars
- where you have to move into the path of oncoming vehicles.

How the examiner will test you

For this aspect of driving there is no special exercise.

The examiner will watch carefully and take account of your

- use of the MSM/PSL routine
- reactions to road and traffic conditions
- handling of the controls.

Skills you must acquire

You must

- show sound judgement when meeting oncoming traffic
- be decisive when stopping and moving off
- stop in a position which allows you to move out smoothly when the way is clear
- allow adequate clearance when passing stationary vehicles. If you have to pass close to them – SLOW DOWN!

Be on the alert for

- doors opening
- children running out
- pedestrians stepping out
  - between parked vehicles
  - round the front of other buses
- vehicles pulling out without warning.

Faults you should avoid

- causing other vehicles to
  - slow down
  - swerve
  - stop
- passing dangerously close to parked vehicles
- using the size of your vehicle to force other road users to give way.

Hazards

Crossing the path of other vehicles

What the test requires

You must be able to cross the path of oncoming traffic safely and with confidence.

You will need to be able to carry out this manoeuvre safely when you intend to

- turn right at a road junction
- enter bus stations or garages on the right hand side of the road.

You should

- use the MSM/PSL routine on approach
- position the vehicle correctly (the width and type of road and the length of the vehicle will affect this)
- assess the speed of any approaching traffic accurately
- wait, if necessary
- observe the road or entrance you are about to turn into
- watch for any pedestrians.

How the examiner will test you

For this aspect of driving there is no special exercise.

The examiner will watch carefully and take account of your judgement of oncoming traffic.

Skills you must acquire

You should be able to

- make safe and confident decisions when to turn across the path of vehicles approaching from the opposite direction
- ensure that the road or entrance is clear for you to enter
- be confident that your vehicle will not endanger any road user waiting to emerge from the right
- accurately assess whether it is safe to attempt to enter the road or entrance
- show courtesy and consideration to other road users, especially pedestrians.

Faults you should avoid

You must not

- turn across the path of oncoming road users, causing them to
  - slow down
  - swerve
  - brake
- cut the corner so that you endanger vehicles waiting to emerge
- overshoot the turn so that the front wheels mount the kerb.

2

Hazards

2 Pedestrian Crossings

What the test requires

You must be able to

- recognise the different types of pedestrian crossing
- show courtesy and consideration towards pedestrians
- stop safely when necessary.

Types of Pedestrian Crossing

Controlled

These crossings may be controlled by traffic signals at junctions

or

they may be controlled by

- police officers
- traffic wardens
- school crossing patrols.

Uncontrolled

Zebra crossings

These crossings are recognised by

- black and white stripes across the road
- flashing amber beacons at both sides
- zig-zag markings on the road on both sides of the crossing
- a row of studs along each edge of the black and white stripes.

Pelican Crossings

These crossings have

- traffic signals which change only after pedestrians have pressed a button on either side of the crossing
- a flashing amber phase to allow pedestrians already crossing to get across safely
- zig-zag lines on the road on each side of the crossing
- a stop line painted on the road for traffic waiting at the crossing

The sequence is

- red
- flashing amber
- green
- amber
- red.

Puffin Crossings

(Pedestrian user-friendly intelligent crossings)

This type of crossing has been installed at a number of selected sites.

They have

- detectors sited so that the 'Red' traffic signal will be held until pedestrians have cleared the crossing
- no *flashing* Amber phase
- traffic lights which operate in normal sequence
  - red
  - red and amber
  - green
  - amber
  - red.

Toucan Crossings

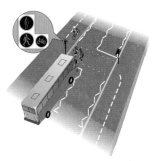

These crossings are mostly found in areas with college or university sites and where there are large numbers of cyclists.

They operate in the same way Puffin crossings do except

- cyclists share the crossing with pedestrians without dismounting
- a green cycle lights when it is safe to cross.

As with Puffin crossings the traffic lights operate in normal sequence

- red
- red and amber
- green
- amber
- red.

Hazards
Pedestrian
Crossings

2

How the examiner will test you

For this aspect of driving there is no special exercise.

The examiner will watch carefully to see that you

- recognise the pedestrian crossing in good time
- use the MSM/PSL routine
- stop when necessary
- are especially alert when crossings are sited
  - near schools
  - at shopping areas
  - on or near junctions.

Skills you must acquire

You must

- approach all crossings at controlled speed
- stop safely when necessary
- move off when you are sure it is safe to do so.

At Zebra crossings

You must

- slow down and stop if there is anyone on the crossing
- slow down and be prepared to stop if anyone is waiting to cross or will reach the crossing before you.

At Pelican crossings

You must

- stop if the lights are on red or amber
- give way to any pedestrians crossing if the amber lights are flashing
- give way to any pedestrians still crossing when the flashing amber light changes to green.

At Puffin and Toucan Crossings

You must

- stop and wait unless the green light is showing
- drive over the crossing only if it is clear of pedestrians or cyclists.

Faults you must avoid

- approaching any type of crossing at too high a speed
- driving on without stopping or showing awareness of waiting pedestrians
- driving on to or blocking a crossing
- harassing pedestrians by
  - revving the engine
  - making the air brakes hiss
  - edging forward
  - sounding the horn
  - overtaking within the zig zag lines
  - waving pedestrians to cross.

Selecting a safe place to stop

What the test requires

When you make a normal stop you must be able to

- select a safe place where you will not
  - cause obstruction
  - create a hazard
  - contravene any waiting, stopping, or parking restrictions
- stop reasonably close to the edge of the road.

How the examiner will test you

At times during the test the examiner will ask you to pull up either

- at a convenient place or
- at a particular place, for example next to a lamp post, or, in some circumstances, at a bus stop.

This is to demonstrate that you could pull up to allow passengers to board or alight safely.

The examiner will watch your driving and take account of your

- use of the MSM/PSL routine
- judgement in selecting a safe place to stop.

Skills you must acquire

You must be able to stop in a safe position by

- selecting it in good time
- making proper use of the MSM/PSL routine
- only stopping where you are allowed to do so
- not causing an obstruction
- recognising any road markings or signs indicating any restriction in good time
- pulling up close to, and parallel with the kerb
- stopping at the correct place when asked.

Faults you should avoid

- pulling up with insufficient warning to other road users
- causing danger or inconvenience to any other road users
- not complying with
  - waiting
  - parking
  - stopping

restrictions

- parking at or outside
  - school entrances
  - fire stations
  - ambulance stations
  - pedestrian crossings.

2

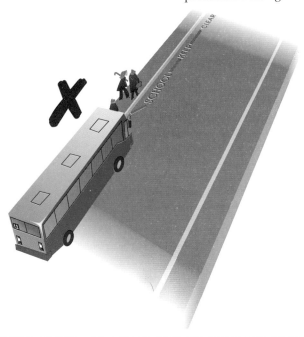

Questions on The Highway Code

2

At the end of the road section of the driving test, you will be asked

- ten questions on *The Highway Code* (with particular reference to PCVs)

- six questions on vehicle safety matters

- to identify six road traffic signs

For examples of questions on vehicle safety – see p 232

The PCV Driving Test Result

If you pass

you will have demonstrated that you can drive a bus, coach or minibus, without passengers, to the high standard required to obtain a licence.

You will be given

- a Pass Certificate (DIOV)

and

- a copy of the Driving Test Report (DLV25) which will show any minor faults which have been marked during the test

- a brief explanation of any minor faults marked. This is to help you overcome any minor weaknesses in your driving as you gain experience.

Sign the back of your driving licence and forward it with the Pass Certificate to the Vocational Licence Section DVLA Swansea SA99 1BR as soon as possible (and in any case within TWO years) to obtain FULL PCV licence entitlement on your driving licence.

After you have passed

you should aim to raise your standard of driving – especially with experience of driving buses with passengers.

Most operators will offer you 'type' training to allow you to get used to the different vehicles on the fleet.

Your trainer should be able to give you further advice.

If you fail

your driving will not have been to the high standard required to obtain the vocational driving licence. You will have made mistakes which either did cause, or could have caused, danger on the road.

Your examiner will

- give you a Statement of Failure including a copy of the Driving Test Report (DLV25) which will show all the faults marked during the test

- explain briefly why you have failed.

You may have made mistakes which you feel were as a result of the "pressure of the occasion." Remember that there will frequently be times when you, as a PCV driver, will be under pressure of one sort or another. You must learn not to let it affect your driving.

You should

- study the Driving Test Report and refer to the relevant sections in this book.

- show your copy of the Driving Test Report to your instructor, who will help you to correct the faults.

Your instructor should not concentrate solely on the faults listed, but will aim to continue to improve all aspects of your driving before you retake the test. Listen to the advice you are given and get as much practice as you can.

Right of Appeal

Although the examiner's decision cannot be altered, you have a right to appeal if you consider that your driving test was not conducted according to the regulations.

- If you live in England or Wales you have 6 months after the issue of the Statement of Failure in which to appeal (Magistrates' Courts Act 1952 [Ch.55 part VII, Sectn.104])

- If you live in Scotland you have 21 days in which to appeal (Sheriff Court, Scotland Act of Sederunt (Statutory Appeals) 1981). See also DSA Complaints Guide for test candidates (Page 215).

Legal Requirements of the PCV driving test

2

The candidate must show that they

- are competent to drive the vehicle in which the test is being conducted without danger to, and with due consideration for, other persons using the road

- are competent to drive the vehicle in which the test is being conducted and in particular can

i   start the engine

ii move off straight ahead and at an angle

iii maintain a proper position in relation to a vehicle immediately in front

iv overtake and take an appropriate course in relation to other vehicles

v   turn right and left

vi stop within a limited distance, under full control

vii stop normally and bring the vehicle to rest in an appropriate part of the road

viii drive the vehicle forwards and backwards, and whilst driving the vehicle backwards steer the vehicle along a predetermined course to make it enter a restricted opening and to bring it to rest in a predetermined position

ix indicate their intended actions by appropriate signals at appropriate times

x   act correctly and promptly in response to all signals given by any traffic sign, by any person lawfully directing traffic, and any other person using the road.

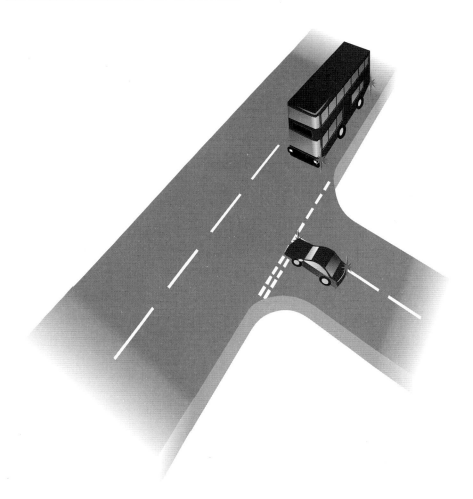

Part 3 of the book looks at driving buses and coaches in everyday situations. It looks at the techniques you should use on the roads to look after yourself and your passengers.

Defensive driving means making allowances. You must always consider the safety and comfort of passengers.

Sometimes, you will have to make allowances for the ignorance of other road users – who, in most cases, will have very little idea of the problems a bus or coach driver faces when driving such a large vehicle.

Defensive Driving

What is defensive driving?

Defensive driving

- means looking after yourself, your vehicle and your passengers
- is based on *planning* well ahead
- requires good observation,
- means keeping in control, and
- means anticipating events.

Know what others are going to do before they even do it!

There are not many excuses for being taken by surprise when you are driving.

Almost every event is predictable.

You must consider and prepare for all possibilities in all situations, especially when you don't know what other road users intend to do.

Remember that you can not brake or swerve like lighter, smaller vehicles can.

Develop

- your awareness (know what is going on all round you at all times)
- your memory of similar situations
- your understanding of what might happen
- your ability to plan ahead
- your anticipation (your experience will soon start to tell you what other road users are probably going to do next)
- being in control (plan **your** actions, don't be forced into situations by others).

You must always drive

- responsibly
- carefully
- considerately
- courteously.

It is up to **you** to remove the 'cowboy' image from other road users' minds. Competition (and sometimes rivalry) between different bus companies offers you a challenge. Show at all times that your standards are high and that you can drive a PCV with skill and safety.

Safety above all

By driving defensively, you will show that you care for the safety of all road users, including yourself and your passengers.

Your passengers trust you. Their safety is in your hands once they are on your bus. Do not betray that trust.

When you are driving

- expect others to make mistakes
- be forgiving. We all make mistakes
- do not 'rise' to aggression.

Aggressive drivers usually come unstuck.

- it is a good idea to let them get on with it . . . somewhere else
- don't be identified with their bad behaviour.

People who drive aggressively often see their driving as a competition. In every situation, they want to 'win.'

Let them 'win' the game because, unfortunately, they are likely to lose the match!

If you let them go first, you will not have 'lost'. . . you are simply refusing to be involved. . .in their accident.

Put yourself in other peoples' shoes

Make allowances for the vulnerable

- children
- cyclists
- horse riders
- elderly pedestrians
- obviously less able drivers
- learner drivers.

In all these examples, the problems arise because you cannot be sure what others might do. Try to prepare yourself for all possibilities.

Control of road space

It is essential that your vehicle is under control at all times.

You must drive it skilfully and plan ahead, so that your bus is always travelling at the correct speed, and ready for your next manoeuvre.

You should never have to do anything at the last minute.

If you get caught out –

you got it wrong!

3

Good examples

Your driving should always be a good example to others.

By driving patiently and expecting the unexpected you will avoid

- giving offence to others
- creating hostility
- provoking others to drive dangerously.

Driving in traffic

Sometimes it may seem to other road users that coach drivers are 'racing' when one coach overtakes another. This is usually because of a coach's load or its speed limiter, and is more obvious on hills.

When this happens, the vehicle being overtaken may sometimes be more powerful and the overtaking vehicle must drop back.

If another coach has started to overtake you but appears to be unable to pass, be prepared to ease your own speed if you think that it would be safer for the other driver to move back to the left.

For this reason you must NOT drive in close convoy.

If you are driving with other vehicles from the same company, DO NOT drive nose-to-tail or look as though you are vying for position with each other along the road.

Competing with other drivers is the opposite to defensive driving and will eventually lead to risking your own safety, or that of your passengers and other road users.

Effective observation

Just looking is not enough!

As a bus driver, you will often have a better view from your driving position than most other road users.

However, because of its size and design, a bus will have more blind spots than many smaller vehicles.

You must use the mirrors constantly – and act upon what you see in them to see what road users around you are doing, or going to do next.

You must constantly be checking down the sides of the vehicle

Offside

- for overtaking traffic coming up behind, or already alongside
- before signalling
- before changing lanes, overtaking, moving to the right, or turning right.

10. Defensive Driving

Nearside

- for cyclists or motorcyclists 'filtering' up the nearside
- for traffic on your left when moving in two or more lanes
- to check when you have passed another road user, pedestrian, or parked vehicle before moving back to the left
- to see where your wheels are in relation to the kerb or gutter
- before changing lanes, after overtaking, moving closer to the left, leaving roundabouts, or before turning left.

You must be constantly checking offside, nearside, offside and so on . . .

Because of your relatively high seating position, you must also be aware of pedestrians or cyclists who may be out of sight directly in front of your vehicle, especially

- at pedestrian crossings
- in slow-moving congested traffic.

Checking the blind spots

In addition, some coaches – particularly those with high side windows make it difficult to see to either side.

When you want to move off, you should open the window and put your head out if you can, to ensure it is clear before you pull away.

Many modern vehicles are fitted with additional mirrors on the left hand side – positioned so that the driver can observe the nearside front wheel in relation to the kerb.

Use them whenever you are pulling in to park alongside the kerb, in addition to checking the vehicle's position when you have to move close to the left in normal driving.

Hitting the kerb or wandering on to a verge can seriously deflect the steering, damage the tyre and result in a 'blowout' later.

Observation at Junctions

Despite your higher seating position, there will still be some junctions where you cannot see past parked vehicles, or even road signs.

If possible, try to look through the windows of other vehicles, or watch for your vehicle's reflections in opposite shop windows.

If you still cannot see any oncoming traffic, you will have to ease forward until you *can* see properly without coming too far into the path of approaching traffic.

Remember that some road users are more difficult to see than others – particularly cyclists and motorcyclists.

Look

Assess

Decide before you

Emerge or enter, then

Negotiate the junction.

Never find yourself having to say, 'Sorry, but I didn't see you coming!'

The Bus & Coach Driving Manual

161

Check and double check

At junctions, check for everything you would normally look for whenever you move off from standstill.

Think once

– Think twice,

– Think bike!

It can also be difficult to predict what pedestrians might do at junctions. Sometimes they might run out into the road, or just step out without having seen you.

Never decide to go after just one quick glance.

Take in the whole scene before you commit yourself to moving out.

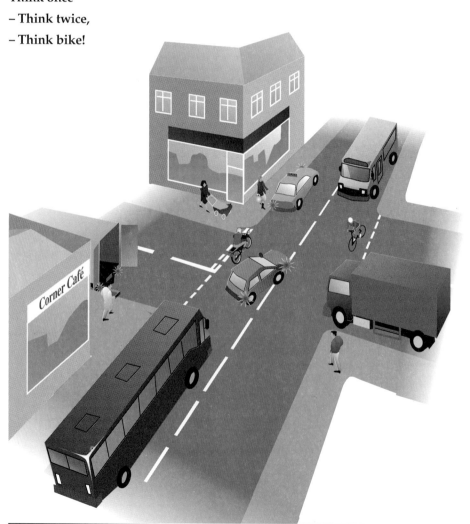

Zones of vision

As a PCV licence holder, you must have better than average eyesight.

As a skilful driver, you must watch the road ahead constantly, to see what is happening and try to work out what might happen next.

You should already know what is behind and next to you. You need to know what is happening at the edges of your vision and note what is happening 'out of the corner of your eye' – and act on your observations.

Check for

- vehicles about to come out of junctions
- children running out
- bikes and motorbikes
- pedestrians stepping out.

Look for clues!

If you see a cyclist ahead glance round to the right, they are probably going to try to turn right into the next road. Be ready for it.

Watch the actions of pedestrians as they approach kerbs.

Elderly people sometimes become confused and change direction suddenly, or even turn back.

Keep a good look out for all horse riders. If the animal starts to behave nervously, allow the rider time **and space** to control their mount.

The noise of the exhaust or brakes from a bus can disturb even a normally calm horse.

Planning ahead

Never drive at such a speed that you cannot stop in the distance you can see is clear ahead

- whatever the weather
- regardless of the type of road you are driving on
- whether you are carrying passengers or not.

This is one rule of safe driving which must never be broken!

- never drive so fast that you cannot see clearly ahead.
- keep a safe separation distance between you and the vehicle in front.
- in good weather conditions, leave at least 1 metre (or yard) per mph of your speed, or a two second time gap.
- on wet roads, you will need to at least *double* the distance, and at least a four second time gap.

The 'Two Second Rule'

You can check the time gap easily. Watch the vehicle in front pass an object – such as a bridge, pole, sign etc. and then say to yourself

'Only a fool breaks the two second rule!'

You should have finished saying this before you pass the same spot.

If you have not, you are too close!

On some motorways this rule is drawn to drivers' attention by 'chevrons' painted on the road surface together with the instruction to keep at least two chevrons from the vehicle ahead.

In busy traffic moving at slower speeds, you may not need to leave as much space, but you must still leave enough distance in which to stop safely.

Tailgating

If you find another vehicle driving too close behind you, gradually ease your speed to increase the gap between you and any vehicle ahead.

You will then be able to brake more gently which means that a closely – following vehicle is less likely to run into the rear of yours.

If another vehicle pulls into the safe separation gap you are leaving, ease off your speed to re-open the gap again.

Never drive at speed, within a few feet of the vehicle in front.

It is not only car drivers in the right hand lanes on the motorway who commit this offence.

Drivers of trucks and buses can sometimes be seen driving much too close behind another vehicle – often at normal motorway speeds.

If anything unexpected happens, an accident could follow. You must not rely on someone else to plan ahead for you. They may not be able to show the same skills as you!

10. Defensive Driving

Look well ahead

Look well ahead for stoplights.

On a road with the national speed limit in force, or on the motorway, watch for hazard warning lights flashing which show that traffic ahead is slowing down quickly.

By planning well ahead, less effort is needed to drive a bus.

By anticipating traffic speeds, you should be able to keep your vehicle moving.

Your fuel economy should improve. This is important and helps a company stay competitive.

Being aware of other traffic

It is important to know what is happening behind you, as well as what is going on in front of you.

Before you change direction or speed, you must decide how any change will affect other road users.

Cars or motorbikes which try to overtake will normally catch up with you much faster than you are moving.

Bus or coach drivers cannot usually see much by looking round, which is why you must always be aware of vehicles just behind you to either your left or right hand side as they come into your blind spot position.

Quick sideways glances

A quick sideways glance is often helpful – especially

- before changing lanes on a motorway or dual carriageway
- where traffic joins from the right or the left
- when coming on to the main carriageway from a motorway slip road

Do not take your attention off the road ahead for too long.

Using the mirrors

You must use the mirrors well **before** you signal or make any manoeuvre

For example, before

- moving away
- changing direction
- turning left or right
- overtaking
- changing lanes
- slowing or stopping
- speeding up
- opening any offside door.

Mirrors must be

- clean and
- properly adjusted.

Looking is not enough!

Whenever you use the mirrors, you must **act sensibly** on what you see.

Take note of what traffic behind you is doing.

Do not allow your vehicle to 'wander,' however slightly, before changing lanes. A bus takes up most of the room available in a lane. You may cause an overtaking driver or rider to think that you are starting to pull out into their path if you move away from the middle of a lane!

3

Approaching traffic lights

At many busy road junctions the road is covered in skid marks. This shows that vehicles have come up to the junction too fast and have had to brake hard.

Traffic Lights on Green

Look well ahead, decide how much traffic is waiting at each side of the junction you are coming to.

Ask yourself

– how long has green been showing?

– can I stop safely from this speed if the lights change?

– if I have to brake hard, will the traffic behind be able to stop safely?

– are there any vehicles waiting to turn left or right?

– how will weather conditions affect my braking?

Signals on Red

You must, of course, stop at red traffic lights. However, you may be able to time your approach to the lights at such a speed as to be able to keep your vehicle moving as they change.

If, for instance, you can see that traffic on the 'other road' has just been stopped, look for clues to suggest whether 'your lights' are likely to go green next.

The professional driver will be able to judge whether a pedestrian phase may interrupt the usual pattern, or if other factors may affect the sequence.

This can be especially important when driving a bus full of passengers uphill to traffic lights. Timing your approach to avoid stopping and moving off again may make your driving easier and your passengers more comfortable.

Traffic lights not working

If you come up to traffic lights which are not working, or there is a sign to show they are out of order, treat the junction like an unmarked junction – and drive on **with great care.** Ensure that your observation misses nothing and be prepared to stop if others assume priority.

Traffic lights 'stuck' on Red

You should not go through a red traffic light by law – unless a police officer tells you to.

Sometimes the phasing goes wrong and the red light shows for longer than it should.

Remember, if you drive on and there is an accident, you will have broken the law.

Never attempt to 'beat' any traffic lights

Don't

• speed up to try to 'beat' the signals – remember what might happen to your passengers if you have to change suddenly from the accelerator to the brake!

• leave it until the last moment to apply the brakes – heavy braking can end up in loss of control.

A vehicle coming across your path may anticipate the lights changing and accelerate forward while the lights are still on red-and-amber. Don't take any risks.

The result of these actions are accidents which need not happen.

Giving Signals

Signal to

- warn others about what you are going to do – especially if this involves a manoeuvre which is not obvious to other road users.

- help other road users.

Road users you need to consider include

- drivers of oncoming vehicles
- drivers of following vehicles
- motorcyclists
- cyclists
- crossing supervisors
- police directing traffic
- pedestrians
- horse riders.

Give Signals

- clearly and in good time
- which are only those shown in *The Highway Code*.

Avoid

- giving any signals which could confuse – especially when you are going to pull up just after a road on the left when another road user might misunderstand the meaning of the signal

- giving unauthorised signals – despite how widely you assume they are understood.

This applies to

– **Headlight 'codes'**

– **Alternating indicator signals.**

Remember, any signal which does not appear in *The Highway Code* is not only unauthorised, but could also be misunderstood by another road user.

Don't signal routinely. Always consider the effect your signal will have on **ALL** other road users.

Using the horn(s)

There are few instances when you will need to use the horn. Using the horn does not

- give you the right of way
- relieve you of the responsibility to drive safely.

Sound it only if

- you think that another road user may not have seen you

- you need to warn other road users that you are there – e.g at blind bends or a hump back bridge.

Never use the horn as a rebuke or simply to attract attention (unless to avoid an accident).

Do not use the horn

- when stationary
- at night between 23.30hrs and 0700hrs in a built up area unless there is danger from a moving vehicle.

Avoid any long blasts on the horn which can alarm pedestrians – if they don't react, they may be deaf!

Part 3 Driving Passenger Carrying Vehicles

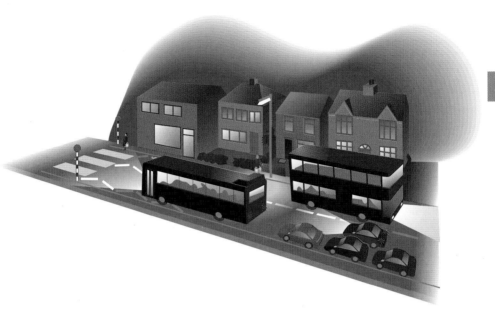

You need extra skills to drive a bus, coach or minibus at night – especially over long distances. There are also added responsibilities for the driver.

You must concentrate even harder than normal. The slightest distraction or break in your concentration can result in an accident.

Many fatal accidents have happened because the driver of a large vehicle either fell asleep briefly or did not see a broken-down truck or car without lights until it was too late.

You need to plan long journeys at night, particularly on motorways with little to ease the boredom. You should also make sure that you get proper rest and refreshment stops.

Above all, you must drive at a speed which allows you to stop safely in the distance that you can see is clear ahead. In many cases, that is within the distance lit up by your headlights or by street lights.

Your eyesight

As a bus driver, you must have better eyesight than other road users – make sure your night vision matches up to this higher standard.

Have your eyesight checked regularly.

Avoid

• wearing tinted glasses

• using windscreen or window tinting sprays.

Adjusting to darkness

When you come out from a brightly-lit area, like a service station, your eyes will take a short while to adjust to the dark conditions.

Use this time to check and clean your lights, reflectors, lenses, and mirrors.

See and be seen!

Difficulties when driving at night

The problems related to driving at night are

• you can see less

• less light (street lights or vehicle lights only)

• dazzle from the headlights of oncoming vehicles

• shadows created by patchy street lighting

• poor lighting on other vehicles, pedal cycles etc.

• dangers created by getting tired.

Lighting up time

Regardless of the official lighting up times (when you must turn your lights on), you should be ready to switch on any lights you may need.

If the weather conditions are poor, or it becomes overcast, don't be afraid to be the first driver to switch on.

See and be seen!

At dawn

Other drivers may have also been driving through the night and may be less alert.

Leave your lights on until you are satisfied that other road users will see you.

Remember, it is harder to judge speed and distance correctly in the half light at dusk and dawn.

The colour of some vehicles renders them less easy to see in the half-light conditions.

By switching your lights on you could avoid another road user stepping, riding, or driving out into your path because they had not realised how close or how fast your vehicle was travelling.

See and be seen!

Lighting

It is essential that all lights are clean and all the bulbs and light units work properly.

As well as being able to see ahead properly, other road users must be able to recognise the size of your vehicle and which way it is going.

In general

- white lights mean that the vehicle
  - will be moving towards you, or
  - is stationary facing you, or
  - is reversing towards you (or is about to do so)
- red lights mean that the vehicle
  - is moving away from you, or
  - is ahead of you and braking, or
  - is stationary facing away from you
- amber lights (which are not flashing) mark the side of a vehicle.

Interior lights

You should also turn on the interior lights if it is gloomy during the day, as well as at night. It helps passengers to move about the bus more easily and safely.

If you are a coach driver, your vehicle may have special lighting for night use. **NEVER** leave the interior of your coach in darkness when you have passengers aboard.

Interior lights have another role in road safety. Newer buses have marker lights along the side, to ensure that they are visible as they emerge from junctions etc.

However, a well lit bus interior is even easier to see!

Auxiliary lighting

High intensity rear fog lights and additional front fog lights must only be used when visibility is less than 100 metres.

3

Unlit vehicles

Only vehicles under 1525 kgs are allowed to park in 30 mph zones without lights at night time.

Be on the alert when driving in built-up areas – especially when the street lighting is patchy.

Although builders' skips must be lit and show reflective plates to oncoming traffic, these items are often either forgotten or are vandalised – watch out for them.

Driving in built-up areas

Always use dipped headlights in built-up areas at night.

It helps others to see you and also helps you to see if the street lighting changes or is not working properly.

Watch out for

• pedestrians in dark clothing

• joggers

• cyclists (often without lights).

Take extra care when coming up to pedestrian crossings – drive at a speed which will let you stop safely if you need to.

Make sure you still obey the speed limits – even if the roads appear to be empty.

Maintenance work

Essential maintenance work is often carried out at night time.

Be on the alert for diversion signs, obstructions, coned-off sections of road etc. when you are driving at night.

Be prepared for temporary traffic lights on rural roads.

Street cleansing often takes place in the larger cities – be on the lookout for slow-moving vehicles.

Driving in rural areas

If there is no traffic coming towards you, you should use full beam headlights to see as far ahead as possible.

Dip your lights as soon as you see the lights of traffic coming towards you. This will avoid dazzling the oncoming driver or rider.

Watch out for pedestrians on the nearside if there is no footpath. *The Highway Code* advises pedestrians to walk facing oncoming traffic in these situations.

Fatigue and tiredness

The smallest lapse of concentration at the wheel can result in loss of control.

There have been several fatal accidents recently which can almost definitely be attributed to the driver becoming over tired.

Take care.

- Do not drive without proper rest periods.
- Keep plenty of cool fresh air moving through the driving area.

- Do not allow the air around you to become too warm.
- Try not to eat a heavy meal before or during a journey.
- If you feel your concentration slipping, pull up at the next safe convenient place.
- Listen to the radio or a tape if you can do so without disturbing your passengers (Don't change tapes while driving, though).
- Walk around in the fresh air before setting off again after a rest stop.

Fog at night

If fog is forecast at night, **DO NOT DRIVE!**

If you drive into fog which becomes so thick that you are unable to go any further safely, you will be a serious hazard to other traffic.

Because of the difficulties of getting a bus or coach off the road in thick fog, it is better not to start out in the first place.

Luckily, the UK rarely sees really dense fogs and smogs nowadays and conditions are rarely bad enough to cancel a scheduled journey.

But visibility can be seriously limited sometimes.

If you start your journey when there is fog about and you are delayed, you will be committing an offence if you drive for more hours than you are allowed because the delay **was** foreseeable!

Overtaking at night

Because PCVs can take some considerable time to overtake other vehicles, you must only attempt to overtake when you can see that it is safe to do so **well ahead.**

This means that, unless you are driving on a dual-carriageway, or motorway, you will have few opportunities to overtake.

Unless there is street lighting, you might not be able to see if there are bends, junctions, hills, etc. which might stop you from seeing a vehicle coming towards you.

If you do decide to overtake make sure you can do so without cutting in on the vehicle you are overtaking, or causing oncoming vehicles to brake or swerve.

Never come up close behind another vehicle before you attempt to overtake it.

When overtaking switch to main beam when you are alongside to improve your vision ahead, provided this will not dazzle approaching traffic (on a dual carriageway, for instance).

Separation distance

Do not drive so close to the vehicle in front that your lights dazzle the other driver.

Make sure you use dipped beam when following another vehicle.

If another vehicle overtakes you, dip your headlights as soon as the vehicle starts to pass you.

Your headlight beam should fall short of the vehicle in front.

Lights on parked vehicles

All buses, coaches, and most minibuses, must have lights on when parked on the road at night, depending on their weight.

Because a lay-by is generally very close to the carriageway, you must still have your lights on!

Unless your vehicle is parked 'off street', such as a coach park, it must be clearly lit by law.

You must park on the left hand side of the road unless you are on a one-way street and it is safe to park on the right hand side of the road.

Breakdowns at night

If your vehicle breaks down, try to stop as far to the left as possible.

If you can, get off the main carriageway without causing danger or inconvenience to other road users, especially pedestrians

Move your passengers as far forward in the bus as you can. This should help to limit injuries if another vehicle runs into the back of your vehicle.

Place a warning cone, pyramid, or reflective triangle at least 50 metres (55 yards) behind the vehicle on normal roads or 150 metres (165 yards) on motorways.

You must be able to warn other traffic that you are there if an electrical problem has stopped the rear lights from working.

Some foreign built buses and coaches have outside fuse and relay boxes on the right hand side of the vehicle.

Do not try to work on the right hand side of the vehicle unless protected by a break down vehicle with flashing amber lights.

Even then, take great care on roads carrying fast-moving traffic.

Many accidents happen at breakdowns. Protect yourself and your vehicle.

3

Assessing the dangers

If your vehicle is in the way of other vehicles or is a possible danger to other road users, tell the Police as soon as possible.

This is particularly important if your vehicle is carrying passengers. You must think of their safety first. If you think that there is a real risk of collision, tell them to get off the bus and wait somewhere well away from the traffic. Explain carefully what you are doing, and ask people to go for help if you need to.

Make sure that you

- know where all your passengers are
- know what they are doing
- tell them what is happening.

Do not leave them yourself unless it is unavoidable

Don't ignore danger signals

If you suspect that there is something wrong with your bus, do not be tempted to carry on driving.

You could end up causing traffic jams if your bus eventually breaks down in an awkward place. A minor problem could turn out to have major effects.

For example, a broken injector pipe dripping fuel onto a hot exhaust manifold may only seem to be a slight engine hesitation to the driver. However, this problem has been known to cause fires in which the bus has been completely gutted.

Recovery agencies

If you are driving long-distance at night especially on 'night trunking', you must know what to do if you break down and need

- another bus for your passengers
- a breakdown vehicle and/or recovery.

If you are an operator, even of just one vehicle, you must be ready for anything that might happen. You cannot leave passengers stranded.

Vehicles which break down on the motorway must be removed promtly for safety reasons.

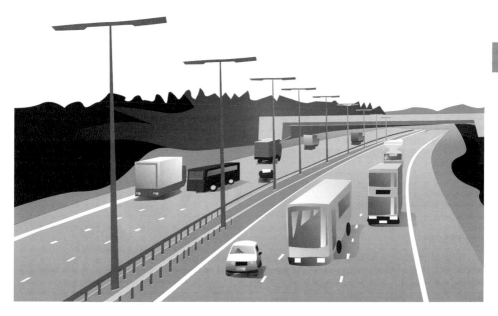

Accident records show that motorways are the safest roads in this country.

However, motorway accidents often involve several fast moving vehicles and result in more serious injuries and damage than accidents on other roads.

Because of the high numbers of large vehicles using motorways many of these accidents involve lorries and sometimes coaches and minibuses.

If everyone who used the motorway drove to the same high standard, many of these incidents would not happen.

You do not have much room to make a mistake when driving fast on a motorway. This chapter looks at the issues you need to consider.

Motorway Driving

Because of the generally higher speeds and the amount of traffic, conditions can change much more quickly than on normal roads.

Because of this you need to be

- totally alert
- physically fit
- concentrating.

If not, you may fail to react quickly enough to any sudden change in traffic conditions.

Regulations

You **must** follow the special motorway rules and regulations.

Study The Highway Code sections on motorways.

Know, understand and follow the warning signs and signals.

Fitness

Do not drive if

- you are tired
- you feel ill
- you are taking medicines which could affect your driving
- you cannot concentrate for any reason.

Any of the above could affect your reactions, especially in an emergency.

Rest periods

You **must** take the compulsory rest periods in your driving schedule.

On long journeys try to plan them to coincide with a stop at a motorway service area.

This is especially important at night when a long journey can make you more tired than usual.

It is against the law to stop anywhere on the motorway, hard shoulder or slip roads for a rest. Nor would this impress your passengers. A driver's tiredness is foreseeable and could not be described as an 'emergency'.

If you do feel very tired, open the windows, turn the heating down, and get off the motorway at the next junction. Even if you are not supposed to stop, it is better than falling asleep at the wheel!

When you get to a service area, have a hot drink, wash your face (to refresh you) and walk round in the fresh air before carrying on driving.

If you eat a large meal before driving, a warm coach, the constant drone of the engine, long boring stretches of road, especially at night, can add to your problems!

Falling asleep at the wheel can happen easily.

Do not let it happen to YOU!

Preparation

Motorway driving usually involves driving long distances at high speeds. Before you drive on the motorway you must make your usual checks, but the following merit particular attention.

Tyres

All of your tyres must be in good condition and be properly inflated.

Some motorways are littered with the remains of tyres which have perished during long high-speed running.

Surveys have shown that the tyres which are most likely to burst are those that are blown up too hard. Make sure the pressures are checked regularly, as you cannot tell just by looking at the tyre.

Inspect inside as well as the outside walls and the treads for signs of wear, damage, bulges, separation, exposed cords etc.

Make sure your vehicle has the same, correct sized wheels and tyres fitted. Smaller wheels will turn faster and may overheat on longer journeys.

Some PCVs are designed to have different size wheels on the front to the rear, but sizes are never mixed on one axle.

Ensure that all tyres are suitable for the loads being carried and the speeds driven. Commercial lorry tyres are not always suitable for PCVs and you should consult tyre specialists who will explain the ratings marked on each tyre.

Use your mirrors to check your tyres while you drive. Check for excessive heat when you stop for a break.

It is surprising how many large vehicles can be seen travelling fast with the driver appearing not to have noticed a tyre shredding itself in a cloud of smoke!

Instruments

Check all gauges – especially any warning lights – air, oil pressure, coolant etc.

Mirrors

Ensure that all mirrors are properly adjusted to give the best possible view behind you.

Make sure they are clean.

3

The simple device of tying a piece of cloth to the mirror bracket works as the air flow causes it to continually 'wipe' the mirror. If you cannot or do not want to do this, you can buy purpose-made devices which look better but do the same job.

In winter make full use of de-misting heating elements if they are fitted to your mirrors.

Keep the lenses and screens of any rear view video equipment clean and clear.

3

Windscreen

All glass must be

clean

Keep all windscreen washer reservoirs topped up, and the jets clear. Make sure all wiper blades are in good condition.

clear

Don't hang mascots or put stickers where they could restrict your view. They will distract you at first, but when you get used to them, they could cause something unusual outside the coach to go unnoticed.

free from defects

Although minor damage to the windscreen is allowed for vehicle tests, the only really safe option is to have the windscreen mended or get a new one immediately.

The effects of a coach windscreen breaking inwards at speed are devastating!

Lights and indicators

By law, all lights must be in working order, even in daylight.

Make sure all bulbs, headlight units, lenses and reflectors are fitted, clean, and working properly.

High intensity rear fog lights and marker lights (if fitted) must also work correctly.

Indicator lights must 'flash' between 60 and 120 times per minute.

Reversing lights must either work automatically when reverse gear is chosen, or be switched on from the cab with a warning light to show when they are on.

Audio and Video equipment

You should not use microphones, change radio stations or tapes whilst driving.

If your bus is fitted with a communications radio or telephone you should only use it whilst driving if it is fitted with a 'hands-off' microphone.

Otherwise find a safe place to stop before using a hand held one.

In any case, do not allow use of equipment to distract you from driving carefully and safely.

Any video or television screen fitted to your coach and used whilst you are driving must

- not be visible to you whilst you are driving
- not be seen from outside the vehicle.

To stop other road users from seeing the screens, you must make sure that curtains are pulled across the windows when televisions are being used.

Fuel

Make sure you either have enough fuel on board to complete the journey, or have the facility (cash, agency card, etc.) to refuel at a service area.

Spray suppression equipment

It is essential that you check all spray suppression equipment fitted to the vehicle before setting out – especially if bad weather is expected.

If wheel arches have sections of anti spray fitments missing, report it as a defect.

Oil

The engine operates at sustained high speeds on the motorway and it is vital to check all oil levels before setting out.

Running low can result in costly damage to the engine and could cause a breakdown at a dangerous location.

Coolant

Similarly, it is essential to check the levels of coolant in the system.

Joining a Motorway

There are three ways in which traffic can join a motorway.

All these entrances will be clearly signed.

At a roundabout

The exit from the roundabout will be made obvious to stop traffic which does not want to use the motorway from accidentally driving on to it.

A main trunk road becoming a motorway

There will be obvious advance warning signs so that traffic which is not allowed to use the motorway can leave the road before the motorway regulations come into force.

A slip road leading to an acceleration lane

Slip roads leading directly on to the motorway will also be clearly signed to stop traffic which does not want to, or cannot use the motorway from getting on accidentally. In many cases the slip road begins as a roundabout exit.

Part 3 Driving Passenger Carrying Vehicles

Effective observation

Before joining the motorway from a slip road try to assess the traffic conditions on the motorway itself.

You may be able to do this from a distance as you come up to the motorway, or if you have to cross the motorway by means of an overbridge, before joining it.

Get as much advance information as you can to help you plan your speed on the slip road before reaching the acceleration lane.

You **must** give way to traffic already on the main carriageway.

Plan your approach so that you do not have to stop at the end of the acceleration lane.

Never use the size or speed of your vehicle to force your way on to the motorway.

Use the MSM/PSL routine – a quick sideways glance may be necessary to ensure you correctly assess the speed of any traffic approaching in the nearside lane.

Remember

Look

(for approaching traffic)

Assess

(the speed of any approaching vehicle)

Decide

(when you can safely build up speed)

Emerge

(safely on to the main carriageway)

Negotiate the hazard

(adjust to the speed of traffic already on the motorway).

You must not

- pull out into the path of traffic in the nearside lane if this would cause it to slow down or swerve

- drive along the hard shoulder to 'filter' in to the left hand lane.

Note: At a small number of locations traffic merges on to the motorway from the *right* – take extra care in these situations.

Approaching access points

After passing a motorway exit, there will usually be an entrance on to the motorway.

Look well ahead and if there are several vehicles joining the motorway

- do not try to race them while they are on the acceleration lane

- be prepared to change your speed

- move to the next lane if it is safe to do so to allow joining traffic to merge.

Lane discipline

Keep to the left hand lane unless you are overtaking slower vehicles.

Unless there are road works, and signs indicate otherwise, PCVs over 12 metres long, large goods vehicles and vehicles towing trailers or caravans are not allowed to use the right-hand lane.

From 1 January 1996 all PCVs over 7.5 tonnes will be banned from using the outside lane of motorways with 3 or more lanes. This is for a trial period and you must make sure that you know about any further changes which may be introduced.

On two lane motorways, all vehicles may use the right hand lane for overtaking.

Use the MSM/PSL routine **well before** you signal to move out.

Do not start to pull out and *then* signal, or signal at the same time as you begin the manoeuvre! Other drivers need time to react.

On a three or four lane motorway make sure you check for any vehicle in the right hand lane(s) which may be about to move back to the left.

Because you are driving a large vehicle some of the traffic coming up behind may be travelling at a much higher speed.

Look well ahead to plan any overtaking manoeuvre – especially in view of the effect a speed limiter will have on the power available to you.

Take special care if you are moving into the centre lane. You must be sure that another vehicle is not planning to use the same road space.

Watch out for signs showing a crawler lane for LGVs. This will suggest a long gradual hill ahead.

If a very large slow-moving vehicle is being escorted, watch for any signal by the police officers in the escort vehicle at the back.

You might need to move into the right hand lane to pass it.

If a motorway lane joins from the right (this only happens in a few places) you should move over to the left as soon as it is safe to do so. The MSM/PSL routine must be used, with careful checks in the left hand mirror and constant awareness of vehicles in the blind spots.

Note: At these specific locations, no offence is committed if a PCV or LGV is at first travelling in the far right hand lane, but they must move to the left at the earliest opportunity.

Separation distance

You must allow more time for everything you do when driving at motorway speeds. Allow

- more leeway than on normal roads
- a safe separation distance.

In good conditions that means

- at least one yard for every mph
- at least a two second time gap.

In poor conditions

- at least **double** the distance
- at least a four second time gap.

In snow or icy conditions you must remember the stopping distances can be **ten times** those in normal dry conditions.

Seeing and being seen

Make sure you start out with a clean windscreen, mirrors, and windows.

Use the washers, wipers, and demisters to keep the screen clear.

In poor conditions, use dipped headlights.

Keep re-assessing traffic conditions around you.

Watch for brake lights or hazard flashers showing the traffic ahead is either stationary or slowing down. (Hazard flashers may be used on moving vehicles to alert traffic to danger ahead).

High intensity rear fog lights must only be used when visibility **falls to less than 100 metres.**

They should be switched off when visibility improves, unless fog is patchy and danger still exists.

Motorway signals

Obey advisory speed limit signs and watch out for matrix lights warning of danger ahead.

Watch for any signs indicating that a lane is closed ahead.

Remember if RED light signals show on the overhead gantries do not go any further in that lane.

Be on the alert for signals telling you to change lanes and be prepared to leave the motorway.

Leaving the motorway

signs will show

At 1 Mile

- the junction number
- the road number
- '1m'

Half a mile from exit

the signs show

- the main town or city served by the exit
- the junction number
- the road number
- '¹/₂ m'

270 metres (300 yds) before the exit there will be countdown markers

- 270 metres (300 yds)
- 180 metres (200 yds)
- 90 metres (100 yds).

Remember that the driver of a vehicle travelling at 60 mph has **60 seconds** from the **1 mile** sign to the exit! Even at a speed of 50 mph, there are still only 80 seconds from the 1 mile sign to the start of the slip road or the end of the motorway.

Plan well ahead so that you can get into the left hand lane in good time.

Large vehicles in the left hand lane may prevent a driver in the second lane from seeing the 1 mile sign, leaving very little time to move to the left safely.

You must use the MSM/PSL routine in good time before changing lanes or signalling.

Assess the speed of traffic well before you start to overtake. This will stop you trying to overtake and then having to pull back in quickly so that you can slow down to leave the motorway at the next exit.

Do not pull across the carriageway at the last moment.

Never drive over the white chevrons which divide the slip road from the main carriageway. If you miss the exit you wanted to take, drive on to the next one.

Occasionally there are several exits close together, or a service area close to an exit.

Look well ahead and plan your exit in good time.

Watch for other drivers' mistakes – especially those who leave it too late to leave the motorway safely.

3

Traffic queuing

In some places, traffic can be held up on the slip road.

Look well ahead and be prepared for this.

Do not queue on the hard shoulder!

Note that illuminated signs have been introduced at a number of these sites to give advance warning messages of traffic queuing on the slip road or in the first lane.

Watch out for indicators and hazard warning lights when traffic is held up ahead.

Use the MSM/PSL routine in good time and move to the second lane if you are not leaving at this exit.

End of the motorway

There are 'End of Motorway Regulations' signs

- at the end of slip roads
- where the road becomes a normal main road.

These remind you that different rules apply to the road you are joining.

Watch for signs advising you of

- speed limits
- dual carriageways
- two-way traffic
- clearways
- motorway link roads
- part-time traffic signals.

Speed leaving the motorway

After driving on the motorway for some time it is easy to become accustomed to the speed so that, when you first leave the motorway, 40 or 45 MPH seems more like 20 MPH.

So

- adjust your driving to the new conditions as soon as possible
- check the speedometer to see the *real* speed.

Reduce speed

Start reducing speed when you are clear of the main carriageway.

Remember that motorway slip or link roads often have sharp curves which need to be taken at lower speeds.

Look well ahead for traffic queuing at a roundabout or traffic signals.

At the end of the motorway be prepared for the change in traffic. Watch for pedestrians and cyclists etc.

Weather conditions on motorways

Chapter 13 covers driving in all weather conditions but there are special considerations when driving on motorways.

Listen to weather forecasts on the radio.

Because of the higher speeds on motorways, it is important to remember the effects that the weather may have on driving conditions.

Rain

The spray thrown up by large, fast moving vehicles can make it very difficult to see ahead.

- use headlights so that other drivers can see you

- reduce speed when the road surface is wet. You need to be able to stop in the distance you can see is clear

- leave a greater separation gap – remember the four second rule as a minimum

- make sure that all spray suppression equipment fitted to your vehicle works.

Take extra care when the surface is still wet after rain – the roads can still be slippery even if the sun is out!

Crosswinds

Be aware of how strong cross winds can affect other road users.

In particular, watch out for these effects

- after passing motorway bridges

- on high exposed sections of road

- when passing vehicles towing caravans, horse boxes, etc.

If you are driving a high sided vehicle, such as a double deck or high floor coach, take notice of warnings for drivers of such vehicles.

Avoid known problem areas such as viaducts and high suspension bridges if possible.

Motorcyclists are especially vulnerable to severe cross winds on motorways. Watch out for them. Allow plenty of room when overtaking **and check the left hand mirror after you have overtaken.**

Ice or frost

In cold weather, and especially at night when temperatures can drop suddenly, watch out for any feeling of 'lightness' in the steering (not always obvious with power steering) which may suggest frost or ice on the road.

Watch for signs of frost along the hard shoulder.

Remember that a warm coach interior can make you forget the real conditions outside.

Motorways which seem to be wet may in fact be frozen.

There are devices which fix on to an outside mirror to show when the temperature drops below freezing point. Some Scandinavian manufacturers fit ice alert warning lights on the instrument panel.

Allow up to TEN times the normal distance for braking in these conditions.

All braking must be gentle.

3

Fog

If there is fog on the motorway, you must SLOW DOWN so that you can stop in the distance you can see is clear.

- use dipped headlights.

Slow down

- use the rear high intensity fog lights if visibility is less than 100 metres.

Stay back

- don't speed up again if the fog is patchy – you could run into dense fog again quickly.

Slow down

- don't hang on to the rear lights of the vehicle in front.

Stay back

- check your speedometer.

Fog affects your judgement of speed and distance and you may be travelling faster than you think!

Slow down

Multiple pile ups on motorways do not just happen. They are caused by **DRIVERS** who

- travel too fast
- drive too close
- assume nothing has stopped ahead
- ignore signals
- ignore the obvious.

You cannot know what is happening ahead if you cannot see!

Even if the motorway matrix signal does not show the word 'Fog', use your own eyes!

Watch for any signals that tell you to leave the motorway.

Watch out for accidents ahead and for emergency vehicles coming up behind (possibly on the hard shoulder).

Police cars may have parked on the hard shoulder with their lights flashing. This might mean that traffic has stopped on the carriageway ahead.

Motorway madness

Motorway Madness is the baffling behaviour of those reckless drivers who drive too fast for the conditions.

It is too late to say afterwards 'I just couldn't pull up in time to avoid hitting them!'

The police prosecute drivers after serious multiple accidents. This is to get the message across to all drivers that they must

Slow down in fog.

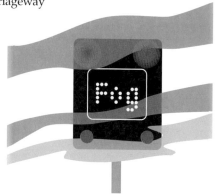

Motorway signals and signs

Motorway signs are larger than normal road signs.

They can be read from further away and can help you to plan well ahead.

Make sure that you know where you are going and how you are going to get there. You must be ready in good time well before reaching the exit you need to use.

Where there are major road works, there may be diversions for large vehicles.

Look for the *yellow*

• square
• diamond
• circular

symbols and follow the symbol on the route signs.

Signals

Warning lights show when there are dangers ahead, such as

• accidents
• fog
• icy roads.

Look out for changeable message warning signs which will warn you about

• lane closures
• speed limits
• hazards
• traffic which has stopped ahead.

Red light signals

If the RED 'X' signals show on the gantries, do not go any further in that lane.

• Be ready to change lanes.
• Be ready to leave the motorway.
• Watch out for brake lights, hazard warning lights showing that traffic has stopped or is moving very slowly ahead.

3

React in good time

If the red 'X' signals show over every lane, stop and wait. You may not be able to see the reason and other drivers may be ignoring the signals, but you are a professional driver. You know what the signals mean and you can demonstrate to other drivers what they should do.

> **Lane control signals ahead**
>
> **lane open**
> **⊠ lane closed**
> **✓ move to left**

Contraflows and roadworks

Essential roadworks involving two way traffic on one carriageway of the motorway are called contraflow systems.

The object is to let traffic carry on moving while repairs or resurfacing take place on the other carriageway or lanes.

Red and white marker posts are used to separate opposite streams of traffic.

The normal white lane marking reflective studs, or cat's-eyes, are replaced by temporary yellow/green fluorescent studs.

A 50 mph COMPULSORY speed limit is usually in force in these places.

This means that if two vehicles coming towards each other crash, there will be a closing speed of 100 mph.

Concentrate on what is happening ahead.

Do not watch what is happening on the closed section of road.

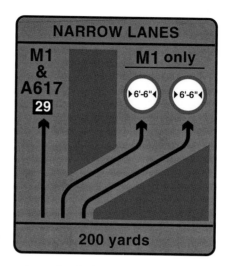

- do not break the speed limits

- keep a safe separation distance from the vehicle in front

- look well ahead so that you do not have to brake hard

- obey advance warning signs which tell you which lanes must not be used by large vehicles

- avoid sudden steering movements or any need to brake sharply

- do not change lanes if signs tell you to stay in your lane

- do not speed up until you get to the end of the roadworks and normal motorway speed limits apply again

Signs

Take notice of advance warning signs (often starting 5 miles before the roadworks).

Get into the correct lane in good time. Do not force your way in at the last moment.

Breakdowns

If your vehicle breaks down in the roadworks section, stay with it. These sections of motorway are usually under TV monitoring and a recovery vehicle (free within the roadworks section) will be with you as soon as possible.

Watch out for broken down vehicles blocking the road ahead.

Passengers want to travel 24 hours a day, 365 days a year. You will need to drive safely so that you, your vehicle, and the passengers in your care always get there safely and with the minimum of hold ups.

This chapter describes the skills you will need to demonstrate when driving in bad weather.

Training and preparation are vital. Only foolish drivers go out in bad weather conditions without being properly prepared.

You must take notice of weather forecasts when they give warnings of severe weather – especially high winds, flood risks, fog, and above all, snow or blizzard conditions.

If a bus or coach gets stuck, the road may well be blocked for essential rescue and medical services, and large numbers of people may be put at risk. If the weather is really bad, cancel or postpone your journey.

In fog, other vehicles could run into your vehicle if you stop or if you have left it unprotected. This chapter is about not taking risks!

3

Your vehicle

Your vehicle must be in good condition at all times.

This means regular safety checks and strict observance of maintenance schedules.

Make sure the vehicle you take out is fully roadworthy.

Far too many cases brought before a Licensing Authority result from incidents caused by a vehicle which has not been looked after properly.

Tyres

Check tread depth and pattern. Examine tyres for cuts, damage or signs of cords visible at the side walls.

Brakes

It is essential that the brakes are operating correctly – especially on wet, icy or snow-covered roads.

Any imbalance would be likely to cause a skid if the brakes are applied on any slippery surface.

If your vehicle has ABS make sure that you understand its use on bad surfaces.

Oil and Fuel

Remember to use the correct grades of fuel and oil in very hot or very cold weather.

Long periods of hot weather will make the oil in engines and turbochargers work harder. You should always allow engines with turbos fitted to idle for about a minute both before increasing engine revs above tickover speed when starting, and before stopping the engine. This prevents bearings from being starved of oil.

When it is very cold, you will have to use diesel fuel 'anti-waxing' additives to stop fuel lines freezing up.

Use of the correct coolant when topping-up prevents dilution of the rust inhibitors and anti freeze components of the liquid.

Allowing a cooling system to freeze will wreck components and possibly crack the engine block or cylinder heads.

Icy weather

Ensure that **all** of the windscreen is clear before you drive away when it is frosty.

Make full use of all heaters and demisters fitted.

If you are driving at night, remember that drops in temperature will cause ungritted roads to become very slippery.

If the steering feels light you are probably driving on ice. Ease your speed as soon as you can.

All braking must be gentle and over much longer distances.

Remember that you must leave more time for the journey because you will need to drive more slowly than usual.

On bad surfaces keep a safe separation distance from any vehicle in front. Leave TEN times the normal stopping distance and drive slowly!

Drive defensively and be careful of other road users getting into difficulties.

Do not accelerate, brake or steer suddenly.

If conditions are really bad do not drive.

No risks are ever justified.

Heavy rain

Although many PCVs have more than one pair of windscreen wipers, you must make sure that you can see clearly ahead all the time. Do not drive if a wiper is faulty. The windscreen must be demisted fully and the windscreen washer bottle(s) must be topped up with the correct washing fluid. This is even more important in winter. It is against the law to drive with frozen or ineffective windscreen washers.

Allow more space for braking – **at least** twice as much as in dry conditions.

Try to brake only when the vehicle is stable (preferably travelling in a straight line).

Do not brake hard or suddenly.

Obey advisory speed limit signs on motorways.

Other road users will have even more difficulty seeing when there is heavy rain and spray, so make sure all spray suppression equipment on the vehicle is safe and is working correctly.

Do not use rear fog lights unless you can see less than 100 metres. They reflect and dazzle following drivers.

Mud

Take care when driving on off-road sites, such as at rallies or festivals.

Do not drive onto a soft surface if you think that your bus might get stuck. You could cause expensive damage to equipment underneath.

If the surface is hard but slippery

• engage the differential lock on the drive axle if one is fitted. This will stop any wheelspin. Remember to switch it out again as soon as you drive on a better surface

• drive at a snail's pace in the highest possible gear with minimum 'revs' and try to plan a course so that you do not have to turn.

It is against the law to deposit mud on the road to the extent that it could endanger other road users.

If you get stuck

There is very limited scope to 'rock' PCVs out of ruts as you might with a car. Clearance underneath is often so limited that the exhaust can be ripped off if the bus has sunk as little as four or five inches.

Seek assistance before this happens. A bar from another vehicle on hard standing, or use of a winch may recover the situation without damage. Once the bus has sunk in only the use of heavy duty jacks and steel sheeting will get you out without further problems.

3

Snow

Falling snow can make it very difficult to see while driving.

Use your dipped headlights and slow down.

Leave a much greater stopping and separation distance of **up to TEN times the stopping distance on dry roads.**

Remember that road markings and traffic signs can be covered by snow.

Take extra care at junctions.

Deep snow is often caused by drifting in strong winds, and can mean that well-known high-level or exposed roads have to be closed.

Listen to the warnings.

Do not try to use such roads if

- **broadcasts tell LGV drivers not to use these routes. The warnings are for buses and coaches too.**

- **warning signs show that the road is closed to large vehicles (or other traffic)**

- **severe weather is forecast.**

Some country roads in exposed places have marker posts at the side of the road which will tell you how deep the snow is.

A bus that has got stuck could

- stop snow ploughs from clearing the road

- delay emergency vehicles

- cause other road users to become stuck

- put passengers at risk.

No risk is ever justified!

Snow ploughs and gritters

Keep out of the way of essential maintenance vehicles.

Do not try to overtake a snow plough or gritter.

You might run into deep snow or skid on an ungritted piece of road.

Keep well back from gritters.

If these vehicles are out, ask yourself whether you should be! The fact that these vehicles are out means that the weather is bad already, or that bad weather is expected.

Deep snow

If your vehicle is fitted with a manually selected retarder system or difflock engage it before going down a hill covered with snow.

If your bus gets stuck in deep snow, engage the difflock to help you get out (if one is fitted). Remember to switch it out as soon as the vehicle is moving and before making any turn.

It is often helpful to keep a couple of strong sacks in your coach to put under the drive wheels if you get stuck, but read the warning on the previous page about getting stuck. Hardened snow can do a lot of damage.

A shovel is often handy if you must go through areas where snow is a problem during the winter.

If the vehicle does get stuck use the highest gear possible to try to get out. Alternating between reverse and the forward gear if possible is a good way of getting moving again when the snow is soft.

Do not keep revving in a low gear. You will only make the driving wheels dig in even further.

If you drive on the continent in the winter, make sure that your coach is properly prepared.

In some countries, you must carry snow chains at certain times of the year. They must be used in bad weather.

You should ask yourself whether your route should go through such conditions.

No risk is worth taking!

Fog

Chapter 12 looked briefly at driving in bad weather conditions on motorways. Whenever you drive in bad weather,

- do not drive in dense fog if you can put off the journey
- try not to drive at all in fog at night
- it is better not to start a journey than to take a risk.

There are not many places where you can find a safe place to park a bus in thick fog. Your passengers will not be very pleased if they have to spend the night in a lay-by.

You must not leave a bus on or near a road where it could be a danger to other road users.

Do not park a bus anywhere in fog without lights.

If you must drive

Slow down

Keep a safe separation distance from any vehicle in front.

If you can see the rear lights of a vehicle in front – you are probably too close to stop in an emergency!

Slow down

Do not speed up if the fog seems to be thin – it could be patchy and you might run into it (or another vehicle) again.

Stay back

Do not speed up if a vehicle comes up close behind you.

Slow down

Keep checking your speedometer to see your true speed – remember that fog can confuse you and make it difficult to know where you are, or how fast you are going.

Stay back

Only overtake if you are SURE that the road ahead is clear – and then only on a dual carriageway.

Just because you have a higher seating position this does not mean that you can see further in fog!

Don't take risks!

Headlights

Use dipped headlights whenever you find it difficult to see.

See clearly and be seen at all times.

Fog lights

Use rear high intensity rear fog lights and front fog lights (if fitted) when visibility is less than 100 metres.

Rear fog lights must be wired so that they work only when the dipped headlights are switched on.

Switch OFF front and rear fog lights when you can see further than 100 metres – but beware of patchy fog.

Keep all lights and reflectors clean and make sure that they are working correctly all the time, particularly in bad weather.

Driving in fog

Do not

• drive too close to the centre of the road

• mix up centre lines and lane markings

• drive without using headlights

• speed up because the fog seems to be thin

• use full beam when following another vehicle. You will make it more difficult for the other driver to see by casting shadows and causing glare in the mirror.

A large vehicle travelling in front of you may punch a hole through the fog – making it seem thinner than it really is. Don't begin to overtake and then realise there is a problem.

Reflective studs

The colours of reflective studs or 'cats-eyes' are

• red on the left hand edge of carriageways

• white to show lane markings

• amber at the right hand edge of the carriageway and the centre reservation

• green at slip roads and lay-bys.

On some country roads there are black and white marker posts with red reflectors on the left hand side, and white reflectors on the right hand side of the road.

These are all designed to help you know where you are on the road.

3

High winds

In bad weather it is a good idea to listen to, watch, or read the weather forecast if you are going to drive

- a double deck bus or coach
- a high floor coach
- a light or empty bus, coach or minibus.

If you have to drive on roads which often have strong winds such as

- high bridges
- high-level roads
- exposed viaducts
- exposed stretches of motorway

listen to advance warnings

- the road may be closed to certain large vehicles
- there may be delays due to lanes being closed (This is done on high bridges to make empty 'buffer' lanes for when large vehicles are blown off course)
- you may need to use another route.

If you ignore the warnings, you could put your vehicle and its passengers at risk. If there is an accident, your passengers could be injured, you could be proved negligent and be prosecuted and convicted.

Don't take risks

Remember that ferry crossings will be affected by very strong winds. There could be delays or cancellations, so it is a good idea to check before setting off.

Watch out for signs warning of high winds.

Beware of fallen trees or damaged branches.

Effects on other road users

When it is very windy, other road users will probably be affected

- when they overtake you
- when you overtake them.

Check your mirrors to see that they are still in control when you are passing (and have passed) one another.

Watch out for vehicles or motorcyclists 'wandering' into your lane.

Do not ignore warnings of severe winds.

You cannot afford to take risks!

The word accident is often used wrongly. An accident is something that happens by chance, or because something which could not have been foreseen has happened.

But most road traffic accidents (RTAs) happen because drivers have made a mistake, failed to see or act on changes in road and traffic conditions or have 'pushed their luck'!

There will be less risk if you drive defensively.

If you are involved in, or have to stop at an accident, this chapter tells you what you should do to stop any one else from getting hurt.

Even in the best systems there will be breakdowns sometimes. The chapter also tells you what to do if your PCV breaks down. Your own and other peoples' safety must be your first concern.

Road Traffic Accidents

If your vehicle is involved in an accident

You must stop.

It is against the law not to.

Sometimes, the driver of a large vehicle does not know that something has happened, especially at night. Stay alert.

You must always try to predict what other road users will do while driving.

You must understand how your vehicle will affect vulnerable road users such as cyclists, pedestrians, and motor cyclists.

Pedestrians at the edge of the kerb and cyclists are more vulnerable to being hit by your mirrors or drawn under your wheels.

Use your imagination, assess every risk and eliminate it.

You can remove most of the accident risk from your own driving by

- concentrating
- staying alert
- being fully fit
- observing changes in traffic conditions
- planning well ahead
- driving at a safe speed to suit the road, traffic, and weather conditions
- keeping your vehicle in good overall condition
- making sure that any passengers don't distract you
- driving safely and sensibly
- not rushing
- not needing to act quickly.

Taking care of your passengers

You must do everything you can to protect your passengers if there has already been an accident.

Decide if there is any further danger and how best to reduce the risk.

Tell passengers what is happening

- without upsetting them further
- by only giving them accurate information which they need to know.

Decide whether it is appropriate for passengers to

- stay where they are
- move to a safer position in the bus if they are able (e.g. to the front if there is a further risk that something might run into the back)
- get off the bus carefully and wait in a safe place (which you must explain).

If you cannot supervise the movement of your passengers, ask someone responsible to do it for you. You must not let people wander around. They will get in the way of the emergency services.

People with medical qualifications will come forward if they can help.

At an accident scene

If you are one of the first to get to an accident what you do could be vital.

You must ensure that you or others

- warn other traffic by using hazard warning lights, beacons, cones, advance warning triangles etc.

- check that there are no naked flames or take the correct action if there are

- make sure someone telephones 999, giving full details of what has happened

- check that all the lights can be seen if hazard flashers are in use. If other road users think that your vehicle is going to pull out or turn, it could make things worse.

Dealing with injuries

If any injured people are not in any immediate danger, it might be best to keep them still until the emergency services arrive.

Be extremely careful about moving casualties – it could prove fatal.

You should

- move any apparently uninjured people away from the vehicles to a safe place

- if anyone is unconscious, give First Aid as described on page 204

- remember that a person who does not seem to be injured may be suffering from shock

- keep casualties warm and do not give anything to eat or drink

- give the FACTS to medical staff when they get there (not what you think is wrong with someone).

3

Accidents on the motorway

Because of the higher speeds, there is more danger of an accident turning into a serious incident. You must inform the motorway police and emergency services as quickly as you can.

- use the nearest emergency telephone
- do not cross the carriageway to get to an emergency telephone
- try to warn oncoming traffic, but do not endanger yourself
- move any uninjured people well away from the main carriageway on to an embankment etc
- watch out for emergency vehicles coming up the hard shoulder.

Hazardous materials

If an accident involves a vehicle displaying either a hazard warning information plate or plain orange rectangle.

- give the emergency services as much information about the labels and any other markings as you can
- if there is an emergency telephone number on the plate of a vehicle involved in any spillage, contact the number given
- keep well away from such a vehicle unless you have to save life
- even then, you must beware of any liquids, dusts or vapours – no matter how small the amount may appear to be. People have been seriously injured from just a fine spray of corrosive fluid leaking from a pinhole puncture in a tanker.

If you are involved in an accident you must

- STOP: It is against the law not to
- tell the police as soon as possible, and in any case within 24 hours
  - if anybody is injured
  - if you damage another vehicle or property and the owner is not there or cannot be found
  - if the accident involves any of the animals specified in law
- produce your insurance documents, driving licence, and give your name and address to any police officer who may need it
- give these details to any other road user involved in the accident if they have grounds to ask for them.

Producing documents

If you cannot show your documents at the time, whether anyone is injured or not, you should report the accident to the police as soon as you can, and in any case, within 24 hours.

The police may ask you to bring your documents to the police station of your choice within seven days **or as soon as is reasonably possible if you are going out of the country.**

- Exchange details with any other driver or road user involved in accident.
- Get names and addresses of any witnesses who SAW the accident.

Taking notes at the scene

So that you have the information when you need it you should try to make a note of

- the time
- the place
- street names
- vehicle registration numbers
- weather conditions
- lighting (if applicable)
- any road signs or road markings
- road conditions

- damage to vehicles or property*
- traffic lights (colour at the time)
- any indicator signals or warning (horn)
- any statements made by other people involved
- any skid marks, debris,etc.

* See page 27 for details about what you should do if you hit a railway bridge.

First Aid on the road

Buses and coaches must carry First Aid equipment by law.

You must know

- where it is
- how to get it out (if it is kept behind glass or in a safety compartment)
- what is in it
- how and when to use it.

Learn First Aid

There are courses available from

- the St. John Ambulance Association and Brigade
- St. Andrew's Ambulance Association
- the British Red Cross Society.

As a professional driver it is a good idea to get some First Aid training. It could help save a life!

The following information might help, but there is no substitute for proper training.

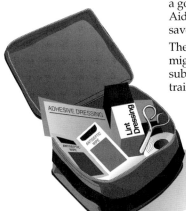

Accident victims

Unconscious

It is vital that you take action within the first three minutes of an incident if you are to save a casualty.

Remember: ABC

- The Airway must be cleared of any blockage and kept open
- Breathing must be started and kept going
- Blood Circulation must be kept going and severe bleeding stopped.

Breathing stopped

Get breathing started again.

- Remove any blockage such as false teeth, chewing gum etc.
- Tilt the victim's head tilted backwards

Breathing should start and the colour should come back.

If not

- pinch the casualty's nostrils together, and blow into the mouth until the chest rises. If the casualty's face is covered in blood, use a clean piece of material, such as a handkerchief, to act as a shield
- let your mouth surround the mouth **and** nose of small children and babies and blow **very gently**
- take your mouth away and wait for the chest to fall
- move your head away, then repeat regularly once every four seconds until the casualty starts to breathe again and can carry on breathing without help.

Do not give up!

Never assume someone is dead.

Keep giving mouth to mouth resuscitation until medical help comes.

Unconscious and breathing

Warning: If you suspect a head injury, do not move the casualty if at all possible until medical help comes.

Only move the casualty if they are in danger of further injury.

If breathing becomes difficult or stops, follow the steps above.

It is vital to obtain skilled medical help as soon as possible.

Make sure someone dials 999

Warning: Do not try to take off a crash helmet unless absolutely essential – you could give a motorcyclist even more serious injuries.

Bleeding

Put firm pressure on the wound without pressing on anything which may be caught in or be sticking out from the wound.

Use the cleanest material available.

Fasten a pad with a bandage or length of cloth.

If a limb is bleeding but not broken, raise it to reduce the flow of blood.

Remember that if you restrict circulation for more than a short time, you could cause long-term injuries.

Dealing with shock

You might not be able to see the immediate effects of shock.

However, quick treatment can help to deal with shock.

- **Do not give the casualty anything to eat or drink.**

- tell the casualty confidently that they will be alright. Keep checking them

- keep any casualties warm and make them as comfortable as you can

- talk firmly and quietly to anyone who is hysterical

- do not let them run into other traffic

- try not to leave anyone alone

- do not move the casualty unless you have to

- if a casualty **does** need to be moved for their own safety, be careful not to make their injuries worse, especially if you put them in the recovery position.

Electric shock

In an accident a vehicle might hit overhead cables or electrical supplies to traffic bollards, traffic lights, or street lights.

Make a quick check before trying to get someone out of a vehicle.

Do not touch any person who is obviously in contact with live electricity unless you can use something which does not conduct – such as a dry sweeping brush etc. You must not try to give First Aid until contact has been broken.

3

Fire

Fire can occur on buses, coaches and minibuses in a number of locations

- engine
- passenger areas
- kitchens and serveries
- toilets
- crew sleeping accommodation
- luggage lockers
- transmission
- tyres
- fuel system
- electrical circuits.

It is vital that any outbreak is tackled without delay.

A vehicle can be destroyed by fire within an alarmingly short space of time.

So that you do not put others in danger you must

- stop as quickly and safely as possible if you find a fire or think that there is one
- get everyone off the bus as quickly as possible. Tell them to stand in a safe place
- dial 999 yourself or get someone else to do it **immediately**
- if you can do so safely, tackle the source with a **suitable** fire extinguisher.

Hazardous materials

If the fire involves a vehicle carrying hazardous materials

- the driver must have been given training to deal with such an emergency. Follow his advice
- the vehicle will carry special fire extinguishers
- keep the public and other traffic well away from the fire

- try to reduce the danger to the surroundings by isolating the vehicle if you can
- make sure that someone calls the emergency telephone number given on the hazard warning plate or the load documents immediately
- warn oncoming traffic.

Above all

Stay calm – act quickly.

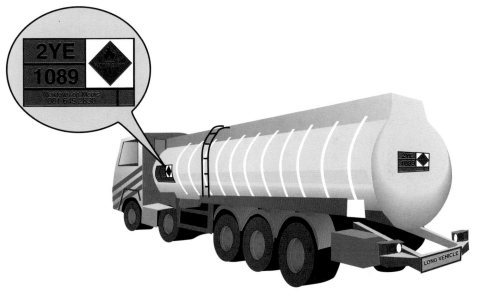

Fire Extinguishers

All PCVs should have at least one fire extinguisher. You must know where they are and how to get them out and use them.

You must know the different extinguishers and which fires they should be used on.

You must not tackle a fuel fire with a water-type of 'soda-acid' fire extinguisher. It will only make the fire spread more.

Most extinguishers smother the source of the fire using inert gas or a dry powder.

Try to isolate the source of the fire.

Do not open an engine housing etc. wide if you can aim the extinguisher through a small gap.

Try not to use a fire extinguisher in a confined space.

If you can,

• disconnect electrical leads
• cut off fuel supply.

There are detailed emergency procedures for dealing with vehicles carrying high risk materials which must be followed exactly. Leave this to the experts.

WATER
UNSAFE
ALL VOLTAGES

CO₂
CARBON DIOXIDE
SAFE
ALL VOLTAGES

FOAM
UNSAFE
ALL VOLTAGES

VAPOURISING
LIQUIDS
SAFE
ALL VOLTAGES

DRY
POWDER
SAFE
ALL VOLTAGES

Driving Standards Agency

Breakdowns

Many PCV breakdowns involve a tyre bursting, commonly known as a 'blowout'.

These are dangerous because they make a bus difficult to control. They also leave debris on the road which causes danger to other road users.

Front wheel 'blowouts'

A front wheel blowout can mean that you will not be able to steer the bus properly.

- keep a tight hold on the steering wheel

- you should always know if there is anything on the left hand side of your bus

- signal left

- try to steer to the left hand side of the road (or to the hard shoulder on the motorway)

- slow down gradually – **do not** brake hard

- try to stop your bus **under control** as far to the left as you can

- if you need to, put a warning triangle, cones etc., behind the vehicle. Switch on the hazard warning lights if it is blocking part of the road.

If you do not brake hard or steer quickly, you should be able to stop the bus without skidding.

Rear wheel 'blowouts'

If a rear tyre bursts you might not notice that it has happened. This is because most large vehicles have twin rear wheels.

However, the ride will become bumpy and, if you carry on driving, the second tyre on that side of the axle will probably burst because it is not designed to run on its own.

Always try to find out what is causing odd handling.

If a rear tyre bursts, you should follow the same procedure as for when a front tyre bursts. However, a rear tyre 'blowout' usually has less effect on the steering.

Breakdowns on the motorway

- try to get the vehicle as far to the left as you can

- do not try to carry out minor repairs on the motorway

- put a warning triangle or cones about 140 metres (150 yds) behind the vehicle

- switch on the hazard warning lights

- make sure the vehicle lights are on at night unless there is an electrical problem, in which case you must ensure that it is protected in some other way (ask another motorist to park behind you, for instance).

3

Emergency telephones

Motorway emergency telephones are free to use. Use them to tell the motorway control centre that you have broken down. They will get in touch with a recovery company for you.

The telephones are 1 mile apart. The direction of the nearest one will be shown by the arrow on marker posts along the edge of the hard shoulder

Do not cross the carriageway or any slip road to get to a telephone.

When you pick up the telephone you will be connected directly to the motorway police control centre.

Face the oncoming traffic while using the telephone.

If your bus has its own telephone make sure that whoever you contact also informs the motorway police, or telephone them yourself.

Part 4 is full of information that you may need as a bus, coach or minibus driver. There are chapters explaining what happens if you are disqualified from driving, what standard of service you should expect from the Driving Standards Agency, locations, addresses and ways of getting more information. It also includes explanations of some commonly used terms.

15. Retesting disqualified drivers

Retesting disqualified drivers

Tougher penalties now exist for anyone convicted of certain dangerous driving offences.

If a driver is convicted of a dangerous driving offence which involves a period of disqualification, all PCV entitlement is automatically lost, regardless of the type of vehicle being driven at the time of the offence.

The decision about whether that entitement can be regained is a matter for the licencing authority.

The options are

- the entitlement may be refused on the grounds that you have shown yourself not to be a fit and proper person to hold a bus or coach driving licence

- the court may require you to take an extended car driving test to regain your category B licence

- you may be required to retake a driving test for each additional category of vehicle you want to drive

- in exceptional circumstances the additional category (ies) may be restored without any further requirement.

Important

You should remember that a PCV driving licence cannot stand on its own.

You must possess a valid full driving licence entitlement for Category B (i.e. a motor car) for your category D licence entitlement to be valid.

If you lose your car licence entitlement you lose your PCV licence with it.

Note. Extended driving tests apply only to categories A and B. There are no extended tests for categories C and D.

212

Applying for a Retest

If you have to take a category B retest you can apply for a provisional licence at the end of the period of disqualification.

The normal rules for provisional licence holders apply.

- you must be supervised by a person who is at least 21 years of age and who has held (and still holds) a full licence for the category of vehicle being driven for at least three years

- L-plates must be displayed to the front and rear of the vehicle

- driving on motorways is not allowed

- PCVs may not be driven if you have only a provisional motor car (Category B) licence.

All driving tests are booked by application to the DSA booking section at the regional office for your area. There are higher fees for extended tests and you must make it clear when you apply which type of test you want.

You can only apply for a provisional category D licence entitlement after you have passed an extended car driving test if the court has directed you to do so.

16. DSA Customer Service

DSA Service Standards For Test Candidates

The Driving Standards Agency is committed to providing the following standard of service for test candidates:

- the national average waiting time for a car test will be no more than 6 weeks

- test appointments will be available within 10 weeks at any permanent test centre

- the national average waiting time for a motorcycle, lorry or bus test will be no more than 4 weeks

- unsuccessful candidates will be offered an oral and written explanation of the reasons for their test result by the examiner at the end of their rest

- test appointment notifications will be issued within 7 working days of receipt of a correctly completed application form and appropriate fee

- 90% of telephone calls to booking offices will be answered within 1 minute

- refund of test fees will be issued within 3 weeks of a valid claim with supporting information

- all letters to DSA, including complaints, will be answered within 10 working days.

DSA Complaints Guide For Test Candidates

The Driving Standards Agency (DSA) aims to give our customers the best possible service.

Please tell us:

- when we have done well

- when you are not satisfied.

If you have any questions about how your test was carried out please contact the local Supervising Examiner whose address is displayed in your local Driving Test Centre.

If you are dissatisfied with the reply or you wish to comment on other matters you can write to the Regional Manager (please see the list of Regional Offices on page 217).

If your concern relates to Approved Driving Instructors you should write to:

The Registrar of Approved Driving Instructors
Driving Standards Agency
Stanley House
Talbot Street
Nottingham NG1 5GU

Finally you can write to

The Chief Executive
Driving Standards Agency
Stanley House
Talbot Street
Nottingham NG1 5GU

None of this removes your rights to take your complaint to:

- your Member of Parliament, who may decide to raise your case personally with the DSA Chief Executive, the Minister, or the Parliamentary Commissioner for Administration (the Ombudsman)

- a Magistrate's Court (in Scotland to the Sheriff in whose Jurisdiction you live) if you have grounds for believing that your test was not conducted in accordance with the relevant regulations, although before doing this you are advised to seek legal advice.

16. DSA Customer Service

DSA Compensation Code For Test Candidates

The DSA will normally refund the fee, or give a free re-booking in the following cases:

- where the appointments are cancelled by us — for any reason

- where appointments are cancelled by the candidate, who gives at least 10 clear working days' notice for car and motorcycle tests, **or 5 clear working days' notice for lorry and bus tests**

- where the candidate keeps the test appointment, but the test does not take place, or is not completed for reasons not attributable to him/her — nor to any vehicle provided by him/her for the test. In addition we will normally consider reasonable claims from the candidate for financial loss, or expenditure unavoidably and directly incurred by him/her, as result of DSA cancelling the test at short notice (other than for reasons of bad weather).

For example, we will normally consider a claim for the commercial hire of the vehicle for the test.

Applications should be made to the Regional Office where the test was booked.

This Compensation Code does not affect your existing legal rights.

List of DSA Regional Offices

DSA Head Office
Stanley House
56 Talbot Street
NOTTINGHAM NG1 5GU
Tel: 0115-955-7600

DSA Regional Offices
Driving Standards Agency

SCOTLAND
Westgate House
Westgate Road
NEWCASTLE-UPON-TYNE
NE1 1TW
Tel: 0131-529-8580
Fee enquiry message
Tel: 0131-529-8592
Credit/Debit cards
Tel: 0131-529-8590

Driving Standards Agency
NORTH EASTERN REGION
Westgate House
Westgate Road
NEWCASTLE-UPON-TYNE
NE1 1TW
Tel: 0191-201-4000
Fee and waiting time recorded
messages
Tel: 0191-201-4100
Credit/Debit Cards
Tel: 0191-201-4108

Driving Standards Agency
NORTH WESTERN REGION
Portcullis House,
Seymour Grove, Stretford,
MANCHESTER M16 0NE
Tel: 0161-872-2333
Fees, waiting times and
information on Saturday tests
(recorded messages) Tel: 0161-
848-0361
Credit/Debit Cards
Tel: 0161-877-5421

Driving Standards Agency
WEST MIDLANDS REGION
Cumberland House
200 Broad Street
BIRMINGHAM B15 1TD
Tel: 0121-631-2020
Fees and waiting times recorded
messages
Tel: 0121-643-3306
Credit/Debit Cards
Tel: 0121-633-4422

Driving Standards Agency
EASTERN REGION
(Nottingham)
Stanley House
56 Talbot Street
NOTTINGHAM NG1 5GU
Tel: 0115-924-2111
Fees and general information
message
Tel: 0115-941-0827
Credit/Debit Cards
Tel: 0115-924-0444

Driving Standards Agency
EASTERN REGION
(Cambridge)
Stanley House
56 Talbot Street
NOTTINGHAM NG1 5GU
Tel: 0122-330-1100
Fees and general information
message
Tel: 0122-353-2111
Credit/Debit Cards
Tel: 0122-330-1113

Driving Standards Agency
WALES
Caradog House
1-6 St Andrew's Place
CARDIFF CF1 3PW
Tel: 0122-222-5186/7/8 and
0122-373-400
Fees, waiting time and
cancellation messages
Tel: 0122-239-5638
Credit/Debit Cards
Tel: 0122-264-1041

Driving Standards Agency
WESTERN REGION
Caradog House
1-6 St Andrew's Place
CARDIFF CF1 3PW
Tel: 0117-922-1066
Fees recorded message
Tel: 0117-929-0602
Credit/Debit Cards
Tel: 0117-975-0075

Driving Standards Agency
SOUTH EASTERN REGION
Ivy House, 3 Ivy Terrace
EASTBOURNE BN21 4QT
Tel: 0132-341-7242
Fees and general information
messages
Kent/Sussex
Tel: 0132-364-7946
Oxon/Hants/Bucks/Berks
Tel: 0132-364-7935
Credit/Debit Cards
Tel: 0132-341-7755

Driving Standards Agency
METROPOLITAN REGION
PO Box 2224 Charles House
375 Kensington High Street
LONDON W14 8TY
Tel: 0171-957-0957
Fees recorded message
Tel: 0171-605-0484
Credit/Debit Cards
Tel: 0171-602-9000

4

DSA PCV Test Centres

Driving Standards Agency Passenger Carrying Vehicle (PCV) Driving Test Centres

Scotland

Aberdeen
Bishopbriggs (Glasgow)
Connel (Argyll)
 (Dumfrieshire)
Galashiels*
Inverness
Kilmarnock
Kirkwall*
Lerwick*
Livingstone (Edinburgh)
Locharbriggs*
Machrihanish (Kintyre)*
Perth
Port Ellen*
Stornoway*
Wick*

North Eastern Region

Berwick*
Beverley
Darlington
Grimsby
Keighley
Leeds
Newcastle
Sheffield
Walton (York)

North Western Region

Bredbury (Stockport)
Carlisle
Heywood (Manchester)
Kirkham (Preston)
Simonswood (Liverpool)
Upton (Wirral)*

West Midlands Region

Garretts Green
 (Birmingham)
Featherstone
 (Wolverhampton)
Shrewsbury
Swynnerton
 (Stoke-on-Trent)

Eastern Region (Nottingham)

Alvaston (Derby)
Leicester
Watnall (Nottingham)
Weedon (Northants)

Eastern Region (Cambridge)

Chelmsford
Ipswich
Leighton Buzzard
Norwich
Peterborough
Waterbeach (Cambridge)

Wales

Caernarvon*
Llantrisant
Llay (Wrexham)
Neath
Pontypool
Wittybush
 (Haverfordwest)

Western Region

Bristol
Cambourne
Chiseldon (Swindon)
Exeter
Gloucester
Poole
Plymouth
Taunton

South Eastern Region

Canterbury
Culham
Gillingham
Hastings
Isle of Wight*
Lancing
Reading
Southampton

Metropolitan Region

Croydon
Enfield
Guildford
Purfleet
Yeading

Note: * Tests are conducted only occasionally at these centres.

Traffic Area Offices

Scotland

83 Princes Street
Edinburgh
EH2 2ER
Tel: 0131-255-5494
Area Covered:
All Scotland and Islands

North Eastern

Hillcrest House
386 Harehills Lane
Leeds
LS9 6NF
Tel: 0113-283-3533
Area Covered:
Northumberland
Tyne and Wear
Durham
Cleveland
Nottinghamshire
North Yorkshire
West Yorkshire
South Yorkshire
Humberside

North Western

Portcullis House
Seymour Grove Stretford
Manchester
M16 0NE
Tel: 0161-872-5077
Area Covered:
Cumbria
Lancashire
Merseyside
Greater Manchester
Cheshire

West Midlands

Cumberland House
200 Broad Street
Birmingham
B15 1TD
Tel: 0121-631-3300
Area Covered:
Staffordshire
Shropshire
West Midlands
Hereford and
Worcester
Warwickshire

South Eastern and Metropolitan

Ivy House
3 Ivy Terrace
Eastbourne
BN21 4QT
Tel: 0132-372-1471
Area Covered:
West Sussex
East Sussex
Kent
Greater London
Surrey

Wales

Caradog House
1-6 St Andrew's Place
Cardiff
CF1 3PW
Tel: 0122-239-4027
Area Covered:
Clwyd
Dyfed
Glamorgan
Gwent
Gwynedd
Powys

Western

The Gaunt's House
Denmark Street
Bristol
BS1 5DR
Tel: 0117-975-5000
Area Covered:
Gloucestershire
Avon
Wiltshire
Somerset
Dorset
Devon
Cornwall
Oxfordshire
Berkshire
Hampshire
Isle of Wight

Eastern

Terrington House
13-15 Hills Road
Cambridge
CB2 1NP
Tel: 0122-335-8922
Area Covered:
Lincolnshire
Leicestershire
Northamptonshire
Buckinghamshire
Bedfordshire
Cambridgeshire
Norfolk
Suffolk
Essex
Hertfordshire

4

Part 4 Additional Information

Other Useful Addresses

Driver and Vehicle Licensing Agency (DVLA) Swansea

DVLA
The Vocational Licence Section
Swansea
SA99 1BR

DVLA
Drivers Medical Branch
Swansea
SA99 1TU
Tel: 0179-230-4000

DVLA
Customer Enquiry Unit
Swansea
SA6 7JL
Tel: 0179-277-2151
Minicom:
0179-278-2756
Fax: 0179 278 3071
(Ring between 0815 and 16.30 Mon-Fri)

The Parliamentary Comissioner for Administration (The Ombudsman)

W K Reid CB, Church House
Great Smith Street,
LONDON SW1P 3BW
Tel: 0171-276- 2003/3000

City And Guilds of London Institute

46 Britannia Street
London
WC1X 9RG
Tel: 0171-278-2468

Department of Transport Mobility Advice and Vehicle Information Service (MAVIS)

TRL
Crowthorne
Berkshire
RG11 6AU
Tel: 0134-477-0456

Confederation of Passenger Transport UK
(previously the Bus and Coach Council)
Sardinia House,
Lincoln's Inn Fields
London WC2A 3LZ
Tel: 0171-831-7546
Fax: 0171-242-0053

Health and Safety Executive Agency

See your telephone book for details of the area HSE office

Enquiry Unit
Broad Lane
SHEFFIELD
Tel: 0114-289-2345

The Traffic Director for London

College House
Great Peter Street
LONDON SW1P 3LN
Tel: 0171-222-4545
Fax: 0171-976-8640

CENTREX (Road Transport Industry Training and Business Services Ltd.)

MOTEC Telford
High Ercall
Telford TF6 6RB
Tel: 0195-277-0441
Fax: 0195-277-0926

Royal Society for the Prevention of Accidents (ROSPA)

22 Summer road
Acocks Green
Birmingham
B27 7UT
Tel: 0121-706-8121

The Road Operator's Safety Council

395 Cowley Road
Oxford OX4 2DJ
Tel: 0186-577-5552

The Coach Operators Federation

261 Stowey Road
Yatton
Bristol
BS19 4QX
Tel:0193-483-2074

Bus and Coach Training Ltd

Gable House
40 High Street
Rickmansworth
Hertfordshire
WD3 1ER
Tel: 0192-389-6607

The National Federation of Bus Users

18 Little Southsea Street,
Southsea Hampshire PO5 3RS
Tel:0170-581-4493

London Regional Passengers' Committee

Golden Cross House
8 Duncannon Street
London WC2N 4JF
Tel:0171-839-1898

The Coach and Bus First Aid Association

D.A. Crewe, Secretary
London Regional Transport
280 Old Marylebone Road,
London NW1 5RJ
Tel:0171-724-5600
ext:21046

The Historic Commercial Vehicle Society

Iden Grange Cranbrook Road
Staplehurst Kent
TN12 0ET
Fax:0158-089-3227

The British Road Federation

Pillar House
194-202 Old Kent Rd
London SE1 5TG
Tel:0171-703-9769

The Chartered Institute of Transport

80 Portland Place
London W1N 4DP
Tel: 0171-636-9952

The British Bus Preservation Group

109 Wellington Street
Peterborough
PE1 5DU
Tel:0173-389-8322

The National Playbus Association

93 Whitby Road
Brislington
Bristol BS4 3QF
Tel:0117-977-5375

The Bus and Coach Working Group (DiPTAC)

The Department of Transport
Room S10/21
2 Marsham Street
London SW1P 3EB
Tel:0171-276-5272

PTE Accessible Transport Group

GMPTE
PO Box 429
Magnum House
9 Portland Street
Manchester M60 1HX

Metropolitan Police Coach Advisory Service

Tintagel House
Albert Embankment
London SE1 7TT
Tel 0171 230 5332

18. Categories of PCVs and Minimum Test Vehicles

Until 1st July 1996

The licence entitlements you will require to drive different types of buses, coaches and minibuses are listed here. You must hold a full (not provisional) category B entitlement BEFORE you can take a test to add an entitlement in this group.

Category	Description	Additional Categories Covered
D	Any bus with more than 8 passenger seats	All PCVs. You may also tow a single axle trailer up to 5,000kg or any other trailer up to 750kg
D1	Small buses with between 9 and 16 passenger seats not used for hire or reward	You may also tow a trailer up to 750kg
D (restricted to 16 passenger seats)	Small buses with not more than 16 passenger seats	You may also tow a trailer up to 750kg
D (restricted to being not more than 5.5 metres (17 feet 9 inches) long	Mini and midi buses with more than 8 passenger seats but not over the length shown	You may also tow a trailer up to 750kg
D + E	Articulated buses and buses towing trailers over 750 kg	D, D1, D1+E
D1 + E	Small buses with between 9 and 16 passenger seats not used for hire or reward with a trailer over 750kg	D1

18. Categories of PCVs and Minimum Test Vehicles

From 1st July 1996

The licence entitlements you will require to drive different types of buses, coaches and minibuses are listed here. You must hold a full (not provisional) category B entitlement BEFORE you can take a test to add an entitlement in this group. You must also pass a test on a vehicle in the category BEFORE taking a second test to add the trailer entitlement (+E). No additional entitlement is required to tow trailers which weigh less than 750kg.

Category	Description	Additional Categories Covered
D	Any bus with more than 8 passenger seats	D1.
D1	Buses with between 9 and 16 passenger seats	none
D + E	Articulated buses and buses towing trailers over 750 kg	D1, D1+E
D1 + E	Buses with between 9 and 16 passenger seats towing trailers over 750kg	none

If the vehicle you use for your driving test has automatic transmission, your licence entitlement will not include vehicles with manual gearboxes.

A vehicle with automatic transmission is defined as a vehicle in which the driver is not provided with any means whereby he or she may, independently of the use of the accelerator or the brakes, vary the proportion of the power being produced by the engine which is transmitted to the road wheels of the vehicle.

This definition includes semi-automatic vehicles where no clutch pedal exists.

Minibuses may be driven with a category B licence entitlement within the UK only provided

• the vehicle is used by a non-commercial body for social purposes only

• the driver is aged 21 years or more and has held a full car licence for at least two years

• the driver provides his or her services on a voluntary (unpaid) basis

• the minibus weighs no more than 3.5 tonnes

Minimum test vehicles

The vehicle you use for your driving test must meet the following requirements.

Until 1st July 1996

All test vehicles in this group must be capable of 80 kph (50 mph)

Licence category	Minimum specification of vehicle to be used for test
Category D	Any passenger carrying vehicle which has more than 8 passenger seats and is at least 9 metres (29'3") long
Category D (fewer than 17 passenger seats)	Any passenger vehicle with more than 8 passenger seats but less than 9 metres (29'3") long Note. You cannot be granted a licence entitlement to drive a vehicle with 17 passenger seats or more, if the vehicle used for the driving test is between 5.5m (17'10") and 9m (29'3") long.
Category D (not more than 5.5 metres (17'10") long)	Any passenger vehicle with more than 8 passenger seats but shorter than 5.5 metres (17'10") long
Category D1	Until 1 July 1996 this category will be granted as an additional entitlement when a test is taken in any of the categories above, or in a category B vehicle (provided the age requirements are met).
Automatic gearboxes	If a vehicle used on test has an automatic gearbox (as defined on the previous page) your entitlement will be limited to vehicles with automatic gearboxes
Towing Trailers (+E)	If you wish to have an entitlement to tow a trailer behind a bus in one of the above categories, you must tow a trailer heavier than 750kgs behind the vehicle you use throughout the driving test. If you already have a C+E entitlement this requirement is waived.

Minimum test vehicles

After 1st July 1996

All test vehicles in this group must be capable of 80 kph (50 mph)

Licence category	Minimum specification of vehicle to be used for test
Category D	Any passenger carrying vehicle with more than 8 passenger seats and at least 9 metres (29'3") long
Category D1	Any passenger carrying vehicle with 9 to 16 passenger seats and up to 9 metres (29'3") long
Towing trailers (+E)	If you wish to have an entitlement to tow a trailer behind a bus in one of the above categories, you must tow a trailer heavier than 1250kg behind the vehicle you use throughout the driving test. You must have passed a driving test using a vehicle without a trailer before you can take this additional test. If you already have a C+E entitlement this requirement is waived.

PSV Licences held before 1 April 1991

If you held a PSV driver's licence before 1st April 1991 and have not renewed it since that date, you will be issued with a new licence showing all the categories which you are entitled to drive, on one document. DVLA will contact you when renewal is due, UNLESS you have failed to respond to a previous renewal notice. If you are in any doubt, contact the Vocational Licence Department at DVLC Swansea. The address is on page 220.

The previous groups 1,1A,2,2A,3,3A,4 and 4A have been replaced as shown. There is now no separate licence entitlement required for double decker vehicles. DVLC will advise you which new categories of vehicle you are entitled to drive. If you previously held a group 1 licence, you are likely to be granted a Category D+E entitlement subject to a satisfactory medical report and driving history.

You should ensure that the categories you need are shown on your licence before 1 July 1996, or you may be required to take further driving tests to regain your entitlement.

Part 4 Additional Information

Vehicle types and Licence requirements

The details contained in this section are subject to possible changes before the rules come into force. You should check with DVLC if you are in any doubt as to the licence entitlement you require.

After 1st July, 1996 the entitlements you will need for the types of vehicles listed in this book are as follows:

Type of vehicle	Category required	Notes
Small minibus with fewer than 9 passenger seats	B	May be subject to taxi or private hire vehicle regulations if used commercially
Minibus or midibus with 9-16 passenger seats (see page 223)	D1	May be subject to some relaxation of the licencing requirement if used under the community bus permit scheme
Single deck service bus or midibus with more than 16 passenger seats	D	
Coaches with more than 16 passenger seats	D	
Articulated buses	D + E	
'Supertrams'	B	Further qualifications are required to comply with the Light Rail Transit systems regulations
Double deck service buses and coaches (including those with 3 axles)	D	
Historic buses and coaches	D	In some cases, these may be driven with category B entitlement when not being used for hire or reward
Mobile project and playbuses	C	In some cases, these may be driven with category B entitlement
Towing trailers	+E	In addition to vehicle category

There is no requirement to display a special type of L-plate when learning to drive a bus, unlike lorries. You must display the standard 'car type' L-plates on vertical surfaces at the front and rear of the vehicle when driving before you pass your test.

20. Road signs

Road Signs

You must be aware of the specific road signs which relate to buses and coaches. Those illustrated on this page are currently in use.

Only

Priority (Red) Routes

A network of priority (red) routes for London was approved by Parliament in June 1992, as a means of addressing the traffic congestion problems and widespread disregard of parking restrictions in the capital.

The pilot scheme in North and East London has been judged to be very successful. The network of 315 miles of London's roads should be fully operational by mid 1997.

Most Priority (Red) Route controls

- operate between 7am and 7pm Monday to Saturday
- have marked boxes where parking is allowed for limited periods
- have marked areas where loading and unloading is allowed
- prohibit stopping (except in marked areas).

On some parts of the planned network on 'high quality' roads where there is no need to stop, 'Clearway' restrictions will be used to prohibit stopping.

When controls apply. drivers must not stop even just to drop off a passenger, or to 'nip-in' to a shop or their home no matter how short a time it may take.

'Stopping' means halting a vehicle for any reason other than

- when prevented from moving ahead by
  - an obstruction
  - other traffic
  - rule of law
  - break down
  - safety considerations.

There are few exemptions to the 'no-stopping' control when and where it is operating. These are

- buses at bus stops
- 'black taxis' allowing passengers to board or alight
- vehicles displaying an 'orange badge' (but only to allow a disabled passenger to board or alight)
- liveried Post Office vehicles when dealing with letter mail.

Information as to the times of the restrictions will be shown on nearby signs.

Parking fines on Priority (Red) routes attract a higher penalty than on other roads in London.

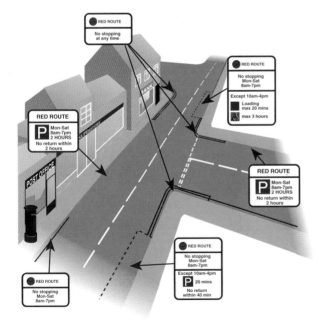

Bus Lanes

Bus lanes are marked on busy roads to assist the flow of public transport.

Use them sensibly and do not be tempted to speed just because the lane is clear ahead.

You may be driving along the inside of stationary or slow moving traffic where pedestrians could be tempted to cross the road. They may not be prepared for you moving faster along the bus lane.

Where the lane has been obstructed try not to get annoyed. It achieves nothing except to distract you from your driving.

Indicate in good time ready to move out and wait patiently for an opportunity.

Be prepared for the end of the lane when other traffic will be changing position.

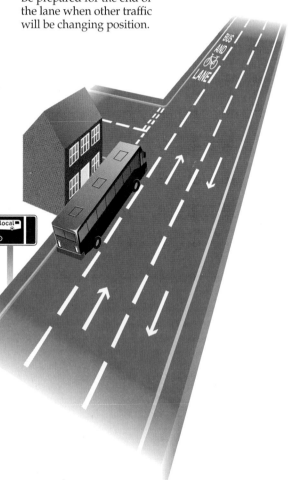

Parking restrictions

Whenever you are driving, whether on stage carriage, on a Private Hire contract, on tour work, or whilst not in service, maintain your professionalism.

Don't stop in places

- where loading and unloading is not allowed

- where you will cause an obstruction

- where you will inconvenience other road users.

Don't park

- where parking is prohibited

- where there is risk of theft or vandalism.

Route planning

Plan your route carefully.

It is never advisable to take 'short cuts' through residential or narrow streets to avoid traffic congestion. You may get stuck, and in some towns weight, size and other vehicle restrictions prohibit you from leaving the main through routes and ring roads, except for access.

The Metropolitan Police operate an advisory service for coach operators. The telephone number is on page 221.

22. Example questions on vehicle safety

1. What should your first consideration be as a PCV driver ?
2. What should you avoid doing when you are driving a PCV ?
3. What safety equipment should you carry on a PCV ?
4. What are the speed limits for a PCV ?
5. What would you do if your coach broke down on a motorway ?
6. What would you do if your vehicle caught fire ?
7. When may you stop on a clearway ?
8. Expain why it is important to have the driver's seat adjusted correctly ?
9. If your vehicle has hydraulic brakes, what does it mean if you need to 'pump' the pedal to achieve adequate braking ?
10. How do air brakes work ?
11. What warning devices are used in PCVs to alert you to low air pressure ?
12. Why is it dangerous to coast downhill in neutral ?
13. How would you be aware of a fault in a power steering system ?
14. Before starting on a journey what safety checks should be made in relation to brakes, lights, steering and tyres ?
15. What precautions should you take if your vehicle is fitted with power doors ?
16. What is 'brake fade' and how can you prevent it ?

These are only examples of questions you must be able to answer. The sort of answers that an examiner would expect on a PCV driving test are given below.

Answers.

1. Your first responsibility is for the safety and comfort of your passengers.
2. You should not eat, drink or smoke or hold unnecessary conversations with passengers or staff, while driving. You should not operate video or audio equipment and should only use communication radios if you can do so safely.
3. Fire extinquisher and first aid kit. (A first aid kit is not a legal requirement on Stage carriage services).
4. The speed limits are

	Single carriageways	50 mph
	Dual Carriageways	60 mph
	Motorways	70 mph (or 60 mph if overall length exceeds 12m or the bus is towing a trailer).

    unless lower limits are shown.
5. Manoeuvre onto the hard shoulder and use hazard lights.

    Inform passengers not to leave the vehicle unless there is danger of fire etc.

    Move passengers forward in the bus if there is room to do so, to avoid injury in the event of a rear end collision. Get assistance by sending someone to use an emergency telephone, or put a responsible person in charge of the coach and its passengers whilst you go yourself.

6. Stop the vehicle as quickly and safely as possible. Stop the engine and pick up the fire extinguisher. Unload passengers quickly and check none are left on board. Ensure that the Fire Brigade is called. Attack the seat of the fire if you can do so safely

7. Never, unless stopping to pick up or set down passengers at a marked bus stop or lay-by; to comply with the law (e.g. red traffic lights); if traffic conditions require you to stop or, if the clearway does not operate for 24 hours, outside its hours of operation.

8. To ensure full control, to lessen fatigue and to gain maximum vision.

9. There is air in the hydraulic fluid or a leak in the system.

10. An engine driven compressor feeds air into one or more storage tanks. When the brake is pressed valves open to allow the compressed air to move pistons mounted near each wheel. The piston rods then move the brake shoes or pads into contact with the brake drum or disc.

11. Guages, warning lights, warning buzzers, indicator flags

12. Because an engine operating at tickover will not allow the air compressor to replace the air lost during braking at a fast enough rate.

13. The steering would become heavier and may not operate smoothly.

14. Brakes
    - check for leaks in the system
    - check pedal travel and handbrake operation
    - test the brakes before going onto public roads

    Lights
    - make sure head, side, rear and brake lamps, reflectors, direction indicators and marker lights, fog and reversing lights are clean and working if fitted.

    Steering
    - no excessive free play at the steering wheel (should not be more than 50mm)
    - power assistance operates correctly
    - steering does not 'wander'

    Tyres
    - make sure that the tyres are not flat,
    - comply with the tread depth requirements (1mm over three quarters of the width of the tyre and the entire circumference)
    - have no cuts more than 25mm long, exposed cords or metal reinforcements and no bulges.

15. Ensure that they are closed when the vehicle is in motion and that no one can become trapped when you operate them.

16. Brake fade is when excessive or prolonged use of the brakes causes them to overheat. The drums may expand away from the brake shoes, and the surface of the lining material on the shoes or pads may become glazed causing a loss of brake efficiency.

You are not expected to give answers that you have learned 'parrot fashion.' The examiner will question you to ensure that you understand what you are saying. The exact words are not important provided that you can show you know what is necessary to operate a vehicle safely.

Glossary of terms

ABS Anti-lock braking system (developed by Bosch) which uses electronic sensors to detect when a wheel is about to lock, releases the brakes sufficiently to allow the wheel to revolve, then repeats the process in a very short space of time - thus avoiding skidding

Air Suspension System using a compressible material (usually air) contained in chambers located between the axle and the vehicle body to replace normal steel leaf spring suspension. Gives even height (empty or laden) and added comfort to passengers (also known as 'road-friendly' suspension).

Axle Weights Limits laid down for maximum permitted weights carried by each axle

BS 5750 British Standards code relating to quality assurance adopted by vehicle body builders, recovery firms etc.

CAG Computer Aided Gearshift System developed by Scania which employs an electronic control unit combined with electropneumatic actuators and a mechanical gearbox. The clutch is still required to achieve the gear change which uses an electrical gear lever switch.

CPC Certificate of Professional Competence Indicates that the holder has attained the standards of knowledge required in order to exercise proper control of a transport business (required before an Operator's Licence can be granted)

C and U (Regs) Construction and Use Regulations which govern the design and use of passenger vehicles

COSHH Regulations 1988 The Control of Substances Hazardous to Health Regulations 1988 place a responsibility on employers to make a proper assessment of the effects of the storage or use of any substances which may represent a risk to their employees' health. (Details can be obtained from The Health and Safey Executive)

Cruise Control A facility which allows the vehicle to travel at a set speed without use of the accelerator pedal. However, the driver can immediately return to normal control by pressing the accelerator or brake pedal. (Rarely fitted to large PCVs but may be found on some minibuses).

Diff lock A device by which the driver can arrange for the drive to be transmitted to both wheels on an axle (normally rotating at different speeds when the vehicle is cornering, for example) which increases traction on surfaces such as mud, snow etc.

DiPTAC Specification Measures applied to PCVs to assist passengers with disabilities (eg bright yellow handrails etc)

Double de-clutching Technique employed when driving older PCVs which allows the driver to adjust the engine revs to the road speed when changing gear. The clutch pedal is released briefly while the gear lever is in the 'neutral' position. When changing down, engine revs are increased to match the engine speed to the lower gear in order to minimise the load being placed on the gear mechanism.

Note. The construction of modern synchromesh gear boxes is such that this technique can cause damage. In such instances, at least one major manufacturer has made it clear that the warranty conditions will become invalid if it has been used. Refer to the manufacturer and the vehicle handbook if you are in any doubt.

Drive-by-wire Modern electronic and air control systems which replace direct mechanical linkages

Electronic engine management system The system monitors and controls both fuel supply to the engine and the contents of the exhaust gasses produced. The system is an essential part of some speed retarder systems

Electronic Power Shift (Mercedes) semi-automatic transmission system which requires the clutch to be fully depressed each time a gear change is made. The system then selects the appropriate gear

Endurance Braking – see Retarders

Fluid flywheel Incorporated in automatic and semi-automatic gear systems, it couples the drive train to the gearbox by use of hydraulic fluid. This allows gear changes, stopping and starting without the need for a separate clutch

Geartronic A fully-automated transmission system developed by Volvo. There is no clutch pedal. Instead, there is an additional pedal operating an exhaust brake

GVW Gross vehicle weight applying to vehicles which includes fuel, passengers etc

HSE Health and Safety Executive

Jake Brake (Jacobs Company) A long established system of speed retarding which alters the valve timing in the engine - in effect the engine becomes a compressor and holds back the vehicle's speed

K Kerb weight Total weight of a vehicle plus fuel but excluding any load (or driver)

'Kneeling' bus Uses air suspension to lower the entrance of the bus whilst stationary for easier access

LA The Licensing Authority is an official appointed to act on behalf of the Traffic Commissioners for a Traffic Area

Limited stop service Bus service operating under stage carriage conditions, but stopping only at specified points.

Load sensing valve A valve in an air brake system which can be adjusted to reduce the possibility of wheels locking when the vehicle is unladen

LNG Liquified (Compressed) natural gas

LPG Liquified (Compressed) petroleum gas

Plate A plate fixed to the vehicle with information relating to dimensions, weights of passenger vehicles and indicating tyre size, maximum axle weight and maximum loaded weight. Certificates are sometimes referred to as 'plates' when required with information relating to tachographs, speed limiters, manufacturer's specifications and height.

Pneumo-cyclic gearbox Semi-automatic gearbox where an electronic or mechanical gearshift operates an air valve system to change gears

Pre-selector gearbox Gear change system where the gears are manually selected prior to use and then engaged by pressing a gearchange pedal. Employs a fluid flywheel and no clutch.

Range Change Gearbox arrangement which permits the driver to select a series of either High or Low ratio gears depending on the load, speed and any gradient being negotiated. Rarely fitted to PCVs.

Red Routes Approximately 300 route miles in the London area which are becoming subject to stringent regulations restricting stopping, unloading and loading.

Regrooving A process permitted for use on tyres for vehicles over an unladen weight of 2,540kg allowing a new tread pattern to be cut into the existing tyre surface (subject to certain conditions)

Retarder An additional braking system which may be

• mechanical – as in the devices which either alter the engine exhaust gas flow or amend the valve timing (creating a 'compressor' effect)

• electrical where an electromagnetic field is energised around the transmission drive shaft (most frequently used on passenger vehicles) – may also be known as regenerative braking when the energy generated is fed back into the vehicles electrical storage system (batteries)

Semi-automatic transmission system in which there is no clutch but the driver changes gear manually

Skip change (Also known as block change) Sequence of gear changing omitting intermediate gears. Sometimes referred to as 'selective' gear changing

Splitter Box Another name for a gearbox with High and Low ratios.

Stage carriage service Local bus service operating according to a route timetable and charging fares based on 'stages' of the journey.

Tachograph recorder indicating vehicle speeds, duration of journey, rest stops etc. required to be fitted to specified vehicles

TBV Initials of French (Renault) semi-automatic transmission system employing a selector lever plus visual display information.

Thinking Gearbox Term used to describe fully automated gearbox which selects appropriate gear for load, gradient and speed etc. by means of electronic sensors

Turbo (Charged) Forced air (from an exhaust driven fan) mixed with fuel to give increased engine performance

Turbo (Cooled) Forced air (fan driven) in addition to liquid engine coolant system also referred to as 'intercooling'

Two speed axle An electrical switch actuates a mechanism in the rear axle which doubles the number of ratios available to the driver

Unloader valve Device fitted to air brake systems between the compressor and the storage reservoir, preset to operate when sufficient pressure is achieved, allowing the excess air to be released (often heard at regular intervals when the engine is running)

VED Vehicle Excise Duty or Road fund licence

Windscreen PCV windscreens are always fitted with safety glass which may be

• toughened – the glass receives a heat treatment process during manufacture so that, in the event of an impact, (stone etc.) the screen breaks up into small blunt fragments reducing the risk of injury. An area in front of the driver is designed to give a zone of vision in the event of an impact.

• laminated – a plastic film is sandwiched between two layers of glass so that an object, upon striking the screen, will normally chip or craze the screen without large fragments of glass causing injury to the driver

LENGTH OF VEHICLE		CONE A	CONE B
Metres	Feet		
4.5	15	225	255
4.8	16	220	252
5.1	17	215	249
5.4	18	210	246
5.7	19	205	243
6.0	20	200	240
6.4	21	195	237
6.7	22	190	234
7.0	23	185	231
7.3	24	180	228
7.6	25	175	225
7.9	26	170	222
8.2	27	165	219
8.5	28	160	216
8.8	29	155	213
9.1	30	150	210
9.4	31	145	207
9.7	32	140	204
10.0	33	135	201
10.3	34	130	198
10.6	35	125	195
10.9	36	120	192
11.2	37	115	189
11.5	38	110	186
11.8	39	105	183
12.1	40	100	180
12.5	41	95	177
12.8	42	90	174
13.1	43	85	171
13.4	44	80	168
13.7	45	75	165
14.0	46	70	162
14.3	47	65	159
14.6	48	60	156
14.9	49	55	153
15.2	50	50	150
15.5	51	45	147
15.8	52	40	144
16.1	53	35	141
16.4	54	30	138
16.7	55	25	135
17.0	56	20	132
17.3	57	15	129
17.6	58	10	126
17.9	59	5	123
18.2	60	0	120

4

Conclusion

Buses, coaches, minibuses and trams have developed rapidly over the past decade or so. Modern vehicles are fitted with 'smart engines' and 'thinking gearboxes', and the driver is surrounded by all manner of electronic circuitry to make the job easier, less stressful and often very enjoyable.

Today's bus driver should have 'service to the customer' as a primary aim and the manufacturers have listened to the needs of drivers, passengers and operators equally when designing their products.

To give a professional service, you need to be a skilled dedicated driver and your driving should be to the highest standards. Your vehicle has made that easier, but the responsibilties you have are greater than they have ever been.

It is in your own interests to keep up to date with changes in requirements as they occur. Ignorance is no defence in law.

Read the informative articles which appear in magazines devoted to driving and remember that by passing the PCV driving test, you will just be setting out on your career.

If you have read this book because you drive a vehicle that does not require you to take a test, or if you took yours some time ago, you have already shown that you understand the need for high standards in your driving. If you are a 'bus enthusiast', you will find you enjoy your interest more if your depth of knowledge and understanding has been increased.

By studying this book you will have made your objective ....

SAFE DRIVING FOR LIFE

26. Index

26. Index

THE DRIVING SKILLS SERIES

ISBN 0 11 551158 X

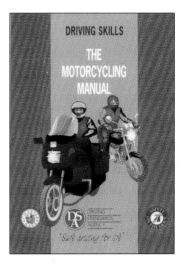

ISBN 0 11 550974 7

ISBN 0 11 551054 0

ISBN 0 11 551192 X

Printed in the United Kingdom for HMSO
Dd298130, C100, 4/95